QAnon and Other Conspiracy Theories

Other Books of Related Interest

Opposing Viewpoints Series

Cancel Culture
Domestic Terrorism
Party Politics
Religion in Contemporary Society
Western Democracy at Risk

At Issue Series

The Deep State
Mob Rule or the Wisdom of the Crowd?
Partisanship
Populism in the Digital Age
Troll Factories: Russia's Web Brigades

Current Controversies Series

Are There Two Americas?
Attacks on Science
Hate Groups
Holocaust Deniers and Conspiracy Theorists
Political Extremism in the United States

> "Congress shall make no law … abridging the freedom of speech, or of the press."
>
> *First Amendment to the US Constitution*

The basic foundation of our democracy is the First Amendment guarantee of freedom of expression. The Opposing Viewpoints series is dedicated to the concept of this basic freedom and the idea that it is more important to practice it than to enshrine it.

QAnon and Other Conspiracy Theories

Kathryn Roberts, Book Editor

Published in 2022 by Greenhaven Publishing, LLC
353 3rd Avenue, Suite 255, New York, NY 10010

First Edition

Cover image: Orlowski Designs LLC/Shutterstock.com

Library of Congress Cataloging-in-Publication Data

Names: Roberts, Kathryn, 1990– editor.
Title: QAnon and other conspiracy theories / Kathryn Roberts.
Description: First edition. | New York : Greenhaven Publishing, 2022. | Series: Opposing viewpoints | Includes bibliographical references and index. | Audience: Ages 15+ | Audience: Grades 10–12 | Summary: "Anthology of curated essays addressing QAnon and conspiracy theories—why they begin, how they catch fire, and how they affect politics and society"— Provided by publisher.
Identifiers: LCCN 2021035618 | ISBN 9781534508392 (library binding) | ISBN 9781534508385 (paperback)
Subjects: LCSH: QAnon conspiracy theory—United States. | Conspiracy theories—Political aspects—United States. | Conspiracy theories—United States—Psychological aspects. | Presidents—United States—Election—2020. | Social media—Political aspects—United States. | Radicalization—United States. | United States—Politics and government—21st century.
Classification: LCC E916 .Q25 2022 | DDC 320.97309/05—dc23
LC record available at https://lccn.loc.gov/2021035618

Manufactured in the United States of America

Website: http://greenhavenpublishing.com

Contents

Chapter 4: How Do People Come Back from Conspiracy Theories?

The Importance of Opposing Viewpoints

Perhaps every generation experiences a period in time in which the populace seems especially polarized, starkly divided on the important issues of the day and gravitating toward the far ends of the political spectrum and away from a consensus-facilitating middle ground. The world that today's students are growing up in and that they will soon enter into as active and engaged citizens is deeply fragmented in just this way. Issues relating to terrorism, immigration, women's rights, minority rights, race relations, health care, taxation, wealth and poverty, the environment, policing, military intervention, the proper role of government—in some ways, perennial issues that are freshly and uniquely urgent and vital with each new generation—are currently roiling the world.

If we are to foster a knowledgeable, responsible, active, and engaged citizenry among today's youth, we must provide them with the intellectual, interpretive, and critical-thinking tools and experience necessary to make sense of the world around them and of the all-important debates and arguments that inform it. After all, the outcome of these debates will in large measure determine the future course, prospects, and outcomes of the world and its peoples, particularly its youth. If they are to become successful members of society and productive and informed citizens, students need to learn how to evaluate the strengths and weaknesses of someone else's arguments, how to sift fact from opinion and fallacy, and how to test the relative merits and validity of their own opinions against the known facts and the best possible available information. The landmark series Opposing Viewpoints has been providing students with just such critical-thinking skills and exposure to the debates surrounding society's most urgent contemporary issues for many years, and it continues to serve this essential role with undiminished commitment, care, and rigor.

The key to the series's success in achieving its goal of sharpening students' critical-thinking and analytic skills resides in its title—

Opposing Viewpoints. In every intriguing, compelling, and engaging volume of this series, readers are presented with the widest possible spectrum of distinct viewpoints, expert opinions, and informed argumentation and commentary, supplied by some of today's leading academics, thinkers, analysts, politicians, policy makers, economists, activists, change agents, and advocates. Every opinion and argument anthologized here is presented objectively and accorded respect. There is no editorializing in any introductory text or in the arrangement and order of the pieces. No piece is included as a "straw man," an easy ideological target for cheap point-scoring. As wide and inclusive a range of viewpoints as possible is offered, with no privileging of one particular political ideology or cultural perspective over another. It is left to each individual reader to evaluate the relative merits of each argument—as he or she sees it, and with the use of ever-growing critical-thinking skills—and grapple with his or her own assumptions, beliefs, and perspectives to determine how convincing or successful any given argument is and how the reader's own stance on the issue may be modified or altered in response to it.

This process is facilitated and supported by volume, chapter, and selection introductions that provide readers with the essential context they need to begin engaging with the spotlighted issues, with the debates surrounding them, and with their own perhaps shifting or nascent opinions on them. In addition, guided reading and discussion questions encourage readers to determine the authors' point of view and purpose, interrogate and analyze the various arguments and their rhetoric and structure, evaluate the arguments' strengths and weaknesses, test their claims against available facts and evidence, judge the validity of the reasoning, and bring into clearer, sharper focus the reader's own beliefs and conclusions and how they may differ from or align with those in the collection or those of their classmates.

Research has shown that reading comprehension skills improve dramatically when students are provided with compelling, intriguing, and relevant "discussable" texts. The subject matter of these collections could not be more compelling, intriguing, or urgently relevant to today's students and the world they are poised to inherit. The anthologized articles and the reading and discussion questions that are included with them also provide the basis for stimulating, lively, and passionate classroom debates. Students who are compelled to anticipate objections to their own argument and identify the flaws in those of an opponent read more carefully, think more critically, and steep themselves in relevant context, facts, and information more thoroughly. In short, using discussable text of the kind provided by every single volume in the Opposing Viewpoints series encourages close reading, facilitates reading comprehension, fosters research, strengthens critical thinking, and greatly enlivens and energizes classroom discussion and participation. The entire learning process is deepened, extended, and strengthened.

For all of these reasons, Opposing Viewpoints continues to be exactly the right resource at exactly the right time—when we most need to provide readers with the critical-thinking tools and skills that will not only serve them well in school but also in their careers and their daily lives as decision-making family members, community members, and citizens. This series encourages respectful engagement with and analysis of opposing viewpoints and fosters a resulting increase in the strength and rigor of one's own opinions and stances. As such, it helps make readers "future ready," and that readiness will pay rich dividends for the readers themselves, for the citizenry, for our society, and for the world at large.

Introduction

> *"QAnon is emblematic of modern America's susceptibility to conspiracy theories, and its enthusiasm for them... The group harnesses paranoia to fervent hope and a deep sense of belonging... To look at QAnon is to see not just a conspiracy theory but the birth of a new religion."*[1]

2020 was a challenging year for the United States. From the global COVID-19 pandemic to the highly contested presidential election between Donald Trump and Joe Biden, the atmosphere was made even more challenging by the intense media coverage of what became known as the QAnon conspiracy theory.

While much of its origins are unknown, QAnon is a widespread and baseless conspiracy theory that truly hit the mainstream media in August 2020. It is believed to have existed since as early as 2017—early on in Trump's term as president—and it is an offshoot of a number of other conspiracy theories from the years before it.

QAnon's followers believe that a cabal of Satan-worshipping Democrats, Hollywood celebrities, and billionaires run the world while engaging in pedophilia, human trafficking, and the harvesting of a supposedly life-extending chemical from the blood of abused children. QAnon's followers believe that former president Donald Trump is waging a secret battle against this cabal and its "deep state" collaborators to expose them and send them all to Guantánamo Bay.

If this sounds like something that has been in the news before, that's because it has, with the Pizzagate conspiracy theory that gained media attention during the 2016 presidential campaign. QAnon evolved out of Pizzagate, but it also has roots in much older anti-Semitic conspiracy theories that will be explored further in this resource.

There are two keys to the rapid growth of the QAnon conspiracy theory and its prevalence during the 2020 presidential election, along with the triggering of the US Capitol insurrection on January 6, 2021: an unmoderated spread throughout mainstream social media platforms like Facebook and Twitter, and legitimization by traditional media entities. Both will be explored in this resource, along with Donald Trump's lasting impact on the social media landscape, even in spite of being banned from all major social media platforms following the Capitol riot.

But QAnon is not the only conspiracy theory to gain traction over the years. There are conspiracy theories for every aspect of society, from aviation to business and industry, espionage, race and religion, medicine, sports, technology, and more. From the Illuminati to the flat-Earth conspiracy theory to the Bermuda Triangle, conspiracy theories are everywhere. But are all conspiracy theories dangerous? Are some of the more innocent conspiracy theories a gateway to even more extremist ways of thinking?

In 2021, it was made clear that the legitimization of the QAnon conspiracy theory was a significant factor in the US Capitol insurrection on January 6, with several members of the mob wearing clothing or carrying signs in support of the theory, such as shirts with "Q" and signs that read "Trust the Plan." But not only that, there were more extreme parties, including the neo-Nazis, in attendance, along with other far-right organizations, like the Proud Boys.

There is also the question of life after a person no longer believes in a conspiracy theory. How does someone go forward? And what can a person do if they have a family, friend, or other loved one who finds themselves believing in conspiracy theories like QAnon. Is it possible to come back? It has already become apparent in 2021 that experts who focus on cult deprogramming are being inundated with requests for people eager to get their loved ones back to the people they were before they believed in the misinformation being spread online.

Opposing Viewpoints: QAnon and Other Conspiracy Theories explores how and why the QAnon conspiracy theory was able to gain such a massive grip on the United States' media and the 2020 presidential election, and the cult and gamelike aspects of conspiracy theories that make them so enticing. Viewpoint authors explore this in depth in chapters titled "What Are the Origins of QAnon?" "What Are the Dangers of Legitimizing QAnon and Similar Conspiracy Theories in the Mainstream Media?" "What Are Other Well-Known Conspiracy Theories?" and "How Do People Come Back from Conspiracy Theories?"

As you read, keep an eye on the publication dates for these articles as well as the timeline before, during, and after the 2020 presidential election. This resource will explore the ways in which these major conspiracy theories could have been stopped early on and will endeavor to explain the ways in which it's possible to stop conspiracy theories from gaining traction in the future.

Note

1. Adrienne LaFrance, "The Prophecies of Q," *The Atlantic*, June 2020.

Chapter 1

What Are the Origins of QAnon?

Chapter Preface

What is QAnon? While it's impossible to know exactly how many people in the United States are aware of the conspiracy theory in any real detail, it is known that the phenomenon exploded into relevance in the mainstream media—both traditional journalism and the most popular social media platforms—in 2020, especially in the months leading up to the highly contested presidential race between then president Donald Trump and his opponent Joe Biden.

The conspiracy theory, which alleges that Trump is the key to saving society from a Satan-like cabal of Democrats, Hollywood elite, and Jewish people, has run rampant around some of the darker corners of the internet, like Reddit, 4chan, and 8kun, since 2017.

While belief in the conspiracy theory knows no political party or affiliation, there is undoubtedly a connection between QAnon adherents and evangelical Christians, along with right-wing members of the Republican Party, primarily in support of maintaining Republican control over Congress and the executive branch.

Similar to the Russian disinformation campaign that impacted the 2016 US presidential election between Trump and Hillary Clinton, QAnon supporters and adherents waged a disinformation campaign in an attempt to influence the 2020 election. Ultimately, they fell into crisis when many theories were disproven by the time President Biden's inauguration rolled around. Those who believed in the conspiracy theory ended up leaving mainstream social media platforms like Twitter and Facebook when the tech giants made the decision to ban Trump's accounts, fleeing to fringe platforms like the messaging app Telegram, which can be seen as a potential gateway for even further and more dangerous radicalization.

The viewpoints in the following chapter examine the origins of the QAnon conspiracy theory—from its start in 2017 as an offshoot of the Pizzagate conspiracy theory, to the first time it was acknowledged publicly by former president Trump at a rally in Tampa, Florida, in 2018, and how it exploded into relevance in 2020 leading up to the election.

They also show the immediate aftermath following the day the 2020 US presidential election was called in favor of Joe Biden and what happened in the weeks leading up to January 6, when QAnon adherents believed that, in spite of the loss, Trump would remain president and would instead be the one sworn in on Inauguration Day.

Viewpoint 1

"Q has consistently made predictions that failed to come to pass, but true believers tend to simply adapt their narratives to account for inconsistencies."

QAnon Is Gaining Traction Around the World

Julia Carrie Wong

In the following viewpoint, Julia Carrie Wong explores how the QAnon conspiracy theory gained traction not just in the United States during the 2020 presidential election, in which former vice president Joe Biden challenged incumbent president Donald Trump, but also around the world. The conspiracy, generated by the anonymous "Q," who allegedly had a high security clearance inside the United States government, shared claims in corners of the internet like 4chan and 8chan and Reddit. Then-president Trump fueled the conspiracy by refusing to either debunk or disavow any of Q's false claims, which centered around Trump's alleged secret battle against a cabal of Satan-worshipping Democrats, Hollywood celebrities, and billionaires, and how the fight would lead to them all being sent to Guantánamo Bay. Julia Carrie Wong is a technology reporter for Guardian US.

"QAnon Explained: The Antisemitic Conspiracy Theory Gaining Traction Around the World," by Julia Carrie Wong, Guardian News and Media Limited, August 25, 2020. Reprinted by permission.

As you read, consider the following questions:

1. What caused the QAnon conspiracy theory to go from anonymous postings on one corner of the internet to a national phenomenon?
2. What are the ways in which the QAnon conspiracy theory can be considered an internet scavenger hunt?
3. Is QAnon actually as prevalent as the media made it out to be during the 2020 election cycle? Why or why not?

To Donald Trump, it's "people who love our country." To the FBI, it's a potential domestic terror threat. And to you or anyone else who has logged on to Facebook in recent months, it may just be a friend or family member who has started to show an alarming interest in child trafficking, the "cabal," or conspiracy theories about Bill Gates and the coronavirus.

This is QAnon, a wide-ranging and baseless internet conspiracy theory that reached the American mainstream in August. The movement has been festering on the fringes of right-wing internet communities for years, but its visibility has exploded in recent months amid the social unrest and uncertainty of the coronavirus pandemic.

Now, a QAnon supporter is probably heading to the US Congress, the president (who plays a crucial role in QAnon's false narrative) has refused to debunk and disavow it, and the successful hijacking of the #SaveTheChildren hashtag has provided the movement a more palatable banner under which to stage real-life recruiting events and manipulate local news coverage.

Here's Our Guide to What You Need to Know About QAnon. So What Is QAnon?

"QAnon" is a baseless internet conspiracy theory whose followers believe that a cabal of Satan-worshipping Democrats, Hollywood celebrities and billionaires runs the world while engaging in pedophilia, human trafficking and the harvesting of a supposedly life-extending chemical from the blood of abused children. QAnon followers believe that Donald Trump is waging a secret battle against this cabal and its "deep state" collaborators to expose the malefactors and send them all to Guantánamo Bay.

There are many, many threads of the QAnon narrative, all as far-fetched and evidence-free as the rest, including subplots that focus on John F. Kennedy Jr. being alive (he isn't), the Rothschild family controlling all the banks (they don't) and children being sold through the website of the furniture retailer Wayfair (they aren't). Hillary Clinton, Barack Obama, George Soros, Bill Gates, Tom Hanks, Oprah Winfrey, Chrissy Teigen and Pope Francis are just some of the people whom QAnon followers have cast as villains in their alternative reality.

This All Sounds Familiar. Haven't We Seen This Before?

Yes. QAnon has its roots in previously established conspiracy theories, some relatively new and some a millennium old.

The contemporary antecedent is Pizzagate, the conspiracy theory that went viral during the 2016 presidential campaign when right-wing news outlets and influencers promoted the baseless idea that references to food and a popular Washington, DC, pizza restaurant in the stolen emails of Clinton campaign manager John Podesta were actually a secret code for a child trafficking ring. The theory touched off serious harassment of the restaurant and its employees, culminating in a December 2016 shooting by a man who had travelled to the restaurant believing there were children there in need of rescue.

QAnon evolved out of Pizzagate and includes many of the same basic characters and plotlines without the easily disprovable specifics. But QAnon also has its roots in much older antisemitic conspiracy theories. The idea of the all-powerful, world-ruling cabal comes straight out of the Protocols of the Elders of Zion, a fake document purporting to expose a Jewish plot to control the world that was used throughout the 20th century to justify antisemitism. Another QAnon canard—the idea that members of the cabal extract the chemical adrenochrome from the blood of their child victims and ingest it to extend their lives—is a modern remix of the age-old antisemitic blood libel.

How Did QAnon Start?

On 28 October 2017, "Q" emerged from the primordial swamp of the internet on the message board 4chan with a post in which he confidently asserted that Hillary Clinton's "extradition" was "already in motion" and her arrest imminent. In subsequent posts—there have been more than 4,000 so far—Q established his legend as a government insider with top security clearance who knew the truth about the secret struggle for power between Trump and the "deep state."

Though posting anonymously, Q uses a "trip code" that allows followers to distinguish his posts from those of other anonymous users (known as "anons"). Q switched from posting on 4chan to posting on 8chan in November 2017, went silent for several months after 8chan shut down in August 2019, and eventually re-emerged on a new website established by 8chan's owner, 8kun.

Q's posts are cryptic and elliptical. They often consist of a long string of leading questions designed to guide readers toward discovering the "truth" for themselves through "research." As with Clinton's supposed "extradition," Q has consistently made predictions that failed to come to pass, but true believers tend to simply adapt their narratives to account for inconsistencies.

For close followers of QAnon, the posts (or "drops") contain "crumbs" of intelligence that they "bake" into "proofs." For "bakers," QAnon is both a fun hobby and a deadly serious calling. It's a kind of participatory internet scavenger hunt with incredibly high stakes and a ready-made community of fellow adherents.

How Do You Go from Anonymous Posts on 4chan to a Full-Fledged Conspiracy Movement?

Not by accident, that's for sure. Anonymous internet posters who claim to have access to secret information are fairly common, and they usually disappear once people lose interest or realize they are being fooled. (Liberal versions of this phenomenon were rampant during the early months of the Trump administration when dozens of Twitter accounts claiming to be controlled by "rogue" employees of federal agencies went viral.)

QAnon might have faded away as well, were it not for the dedicated work of three conspiracy theorists who latched on to it at the very beginning and translated it into a digestible narrative for mainstream social media networks. A 2018 investigation by NBC News uncovered how this trio worked together to promote and profit off QAnon, turning it into the broad, multi-platform internet phenomenon that it is today. There now exists an entire QAnon media ecosystem, with enormous amounts of video content, memes, e-books, chatrooms, and more, all designed to snare the interest of potential recruits, then draw them "down the rabbit hole" and into QAnon's alternate reality.

How Many People Believe in QAnon? And Who Are They?

Nobody knows, but we think it's fair to say at least 100,000 people.

Experts in conspiracy theories point out that belief in QAnon is far from common. While at one point, 80% of Americans believed a conspiracy theory about the Kennedy assassination, a poll by Pew Research in March found that 76% of Americans had never heard of QAnon and just 3% knew "a lot" about it.

The largest Facebook groups dedicated to QAnon had approximately 200,000 members in them before Facebook banned them in mid-August. When Twitter took similar action against QAnon accounts in July, it limited features for approximately 150,000 accounts. In June, a Q drop that contained a link to a year-old *Guardian* article resulted in approximately 150,000 page views over the next 24 hours.

These are rough figures to draw a conclusion from, but in the absence of better data, they hint at the scale of the online movement.

In general, QAnon appears to be most popular among older Republicans and evangelical Christians. There are subcultures within QAnon for people who approach studying Q drops in a manner similar to Bible study. Other followers appear to have come to QAnon from New Age spiritual movements, from more traditional conspiracy theory communities, or from the far right. Since adulation for Trump is a prerequisite, it is almost exclusively a conservative movement, though the #SaveTheChildren campaign is helping it make inroads among non-Trump supporters (see below).

QAnon has spread to Latin America and Europe, where it appears to be catching on among certain far-right movements.

Why Does QAnon Matter?

First, there's the threat of violence. For those who truly believe that powerful figures are holding children hostage in order to exploit them sexually or for their blood, taking action to stop the abuse can seem like a moral imperative. While most QAnon followers will not engage in violence, many already have, or have attempted to, which is why the FBI has identified the movement as a potential domestic terror threat. Participation in QAnon also often involves vicious online harassment campaigns against perceived enemies, which can have serious consequences for the targets.

QAnon is also gaining traction as a political force in the Republican Party, which could have real and damaging effects on American democracy. Media Matters has compiled a list of 77 candidates for congressional seats who have indicated support for QAnon and at least one of them, Georgia's Marjorie Taylor Greene, will in all likelihood be elected in November.

As the hero of the overall narrative, Trump has the unique ability to influence QAnon believers. On 19 August, at a White House press briefing, he was given the opportunity to debunk the

New Heights in Disinformation

Democrats this week called for the expulsion of first-term Congresswoman Marjorie Taylor Greene of Georgia for repeating anti-Semitic tropes and amplifying dangerous—and discredited—QAnon conspiracy theories.

False allegations of mass election fraud—disinformation that Greene perpetuated—helped fuel the deadly Capitol insurrection.

"President Trump did not cause the attack on the Capitol on January 6th," Greene said at a town hall on January 28.

For his part, former president Trump has sidestepped QAnon, claiming he knows little about a movement at the core of his support.

"I've heard these are people that love our country," Mr. Trump said in August 2020.

Disinformation reached new heights in 2020. A recent study showed Facebook users interacted with deceptive posts more than

theory once and for all. Instead, he praised QAnon followers as patriots and appeared to affirm the central premise of the belief, saying: "If I can help save the world from problems, I'm willing to do it; I'm willing to put myself out there, and we are, actually. We're saving the world from a radical left philosophy that will destroy this country and, when this country is gone, the rest of the world will follow."

QAnon believers were jubilant.

Didn't You Mention #SaveTheChildren? What's That All About?

Participating in QAnon is largely made up of "research"—ie, learning more about the byzantine theories or decoding Q drops—and evangelism. Most of the proselytization relies on media manipulation tactics designed to catch users' attention and send them into a controlled online media environment where they will become "redpilled" through consuming pro-QAnon content.

1 billion times in October, November and December—about twice the total leading up to the 2016 election.

"That even when people were increasing their news consumption overall online, their consumption of the set of information from the deceptive sites was even greater," said Karen Kornbluh, who leads German Marshall Fund's Digital New Deal project.

The QAnon world is rooted in a belief Mr. Trump can save society from a cabal of Democratic pedophiles running a global child trafficking ring.

"It was a drug. It was absolutely a drug," said Jitarth Jadeja, a former QAnon believer who said he lost almost two years of his life to the cult.

"You should be really scared, these guys are dangerous. They're more dangerous than white supremacists," Jadeja said.

"It Was a Drug: Capitol Riot Exposes Reach of QAnon Disinformation," by Major Garrett, CBS News, January 31, 2021.

QAnon followers have for years used a wide range of online tactics to achieve virality and garner mainstream media coverage, including making "documentaries" full of misinformation, hijacking trending hashtags with QAnon messaging, showing up at Trump rallies with Q signs, or running for elected office.

A very potent iteration of this tactic emerged this summer with the #SaveTheChildren or #SaveOurChildren campaign. The innocuous sounding hashtag, which had previously been used by anti-child-trafficking NGOs, has been flooded with emotive content by QAnon adherents hinting at the broader QAnon narrative. (It doesn't help that the debate around human trafficking is already full of bogus statistics.)

On Facebook, anxiety over children due to the coronavirus pandemic, a resurgent anti-vaxx movement, and QAnon-fueled scaremongering about child trafficking have all combined to inspire a modern-day moral panic, somewhat akin to the "Satanic Panic" of the 1980s.

Hundreds of real-life "Save Our Children" protests have been organized on Facebook in communities across the US (and around the world). These small rallies are in turn driving local news coverage by outlets who don't realize that by publishing news designed to "raise awareness" about child trafficking, they are encouraging their readers or viewers to head to the internet, where a search for "save our children" could send them straight down the QAnon rabbit hole.

> *"Victory over demons is paralleled with the mass expulsion of undocumented migrants. Others have framed the central American migrant caravans as carriers of diabolic 'witchcraft.'"*

Evangelicals and Conspiracy Theories Combine in Trump's America

S. Jonathon O'Donnell

In the following viewpoint, S. Jonathon O'Donnell shares how increasingly vocal evangelicals have become about the apparent demonic forces active in US politics and American life in general. These theories are centralized around the idea that demons have taken control of commonly liberal institutions such as journalism and academia and therefore frame the advancement of social projects as something in opposition to God's plans. Specific examples are advances in reproductive and LGBTQ rights, along with tolerance for non-Christian religions, especially Islam. With the help of the QAnon conspiracy, there is now a new narrative that God is retaking control of the United States from these demonic forces, bringing life back to something more in line with the views of those in the evangelical faith. S. Jonathon O'Donnell is a postdoctoral fellow in American studies at University College Dublin.

"Demons of the Deep State: How Evangelicals and Conspiracy Theories Combine in Trump's America," by S. Jonathon O'Donnell, The Conversation, September 14, 2020. https://theconversation.com/demons-of-the-deep-state-how-evangelicals-and-conspiracy-theories-combine-in-trumps-america-144898.

As you read, consider the following questions:

1. Why have evangelicals made a connection between the fight against demons and their political affiliations and efforts?
2. What is the connection between the deep state and the perceived demonic control over non-evangelical people in the US and around the world?
3. What are the commonalities between all the "demonized" groups that evangelicals are attempting to fight against?

Are demons active forces in American life and politics? That is what a large number of evangelicals in the US believe and are increasingly vocal about.

Since the 1980s, growing numbers of evangelicals have given the fight against demons a key role in their spirituality and their politics. Known as "spiritual warfare," this views demons as central actors in world politics and everyday life. While often seen as fringe, belief in spiritual warfare is common across denominational lines, including among evangelicals close to Donald Trump, such as Robert Jeffress and the president's spiritual advisor, Paula White.

A key idea in spiritual warfare is that demons don't only attack people, as in depictions of demonic possession, but also take control of places and institutions, such as journalism, academia, and both municipal and federal bureaucracies. By doing so, demons are framed as advancing social projects that spiritual warriors see as opposing God's plans. These include advances in reproductive and LGBTQ rights and tolerance for non-Christian religions (especially Islam).

In a recent article published in the journal *Religion*, I explore how these ideas about demons combine with the wider Christian nationalism shown to be prevalent among Trump's support base. Through a survey of conservative evangelical literature, articles, and television and radio broadcasts released between 2016 and 2018, I analyse how their authors used discourses of spiritual warfare to navigate the changing political reality, and Trump's victory and presidency in particular.

The evangelicals whose works I analyse vary in their attitudes to Trump, from ardent advocates to reluctant supporters. Yet even the reluctant supporters interpret his presidency in terms of spiritual warfare, framing Trump's victory as a divine intervention against a demonic status quo.

Trump's alleged battle against the "deep state" here adopts cosmic meaning, as not only the US government but undocumented immigrants and Black and LGBTQ people are cast as agents of demonic forces.

Divine Intervention

The deep state has become a watchword of the Trump era, a term used by his supporters to depict Trump as an outsider fighting a corrupted political system. The deep state is central to the conspiracy movement QAnon, which depicts Trump as at war with a "deep state cabal" of devil-worshipping cannibal paedophiles.

QAnon has many overlaps with spiritual warfare and its practitioners. It uses similar ideas of religious revival and donning the "armour of God" against unseen foes.

Not all spiritual warriors engage with QAnon. But even for those that don't, the deep state has come to represent broader ideas of demonic control, as demons are imagined as a "deeper state" working behind the scenes. Demons become the source of economic and environmental regulations and of social welfare programmes. The deregulatory ambitions that former White House chief strategist Steve Bannon called Trump's "deconstruction of the administrative state" become imagined as a project of national exorcism.

For many spiritual warriors this project began on election night 2016. Trump's improbable victory stoked narratives of divine intervention. Comparing the red electoral map of Republican victory to "the blood of Jesus" washing away America's sins, one evangelical framed the election as overthrowing "Jezebel," a demonic spirit often depicted as behind reproductive and LGBTQ rights.

Banning abortion is central to conservative evangelical politics. Spiritual warriors often go further, framing support for abortion and same-sex marriage as both causing and caused by demonic control. They portray evil spirits and sinful humans as creating reinforcing systems of beliefs, behaviours and policy agendas. The deep state has become a key representation of these systems.

This spiritual war against the deep state can be understood as part of post-truth politics. While sometimes seen as a politics that delegitimises truth itself, post-truth can also be understood as a destabilisation of mainstream narratives about society. One that allows new narratives to be pushed.

In spiritual warfare, this new narrative is one where God is retaking control of the US from demonic forces. One where God's truth is being reasserted over competing truths, which are reframed as demonic lies. Spiritual warfare here becomes a struggle over competing narratives about what America is, or should be. Dismantling the deep state is part of this struggle. But it is not the only one.

The Demons at Work

Spiritual warfare has also come to frame evangelical reactions to ongoing protests. Demonic opposition to Trump has been positioned by spiritual warriors as being behind events from the 2017 Women's March to the 2020 protests sparked by the killing of George Floyd. Stances on immigrants and refugees are also included.

In one book, turned into a part-biopic, part-propaganda film called *The Trump Prophecy* by the conservative evangelical Liberty University, victory over demons is paralleled with the mass expulsion of undocumented migrants. Others have framed the central American migrant caravans as carriers of diabolic "witchcraft."

Conspiratorial claims that both the protests and migrant caravans were funded by the investor/philanthropist George Soros or the deep state close the circle. They cast demonised groups—such as "nasty" women, Black protesters, refugees and undocumented migrants—not just as agents of corrupt deep state forces but avatars of the demonic deeper state behind them.

Spiritual warriors are often keen to separate the demons they battle from the people they claim to be saving from them. But today such deliverance from evil has been shown to never just be about the spiritual salvation of individuals, if it ever was. It has profound and lasting material consequences for both those individuals and the nation.

By imagining demons behind social welfare, economic and environmental regulations, or legal protections for marginalised groups, spiritual warriors frame the dismantling of these systems as ridding the US of demons. More than this, they frame the people and groups they see as benefiting from those systems as agents of evil incarnate. Only after such people are removed can there be a national rebirth.

> *"The #voterid hashtag has been consistently targeted by Qanon over a period of months, including stockpiling hundreds of memes relating to voter ID and voter fraud in shared accounts on image-file-sharing sites."*

QAnon Deployed "Information Warfare" to Influence the 2020 Election

Elise Thomas

In the following viewpoint, Elise Thomas argues that the relatively small base of QAnon adherents and followers was able to overtake the social media landscape during the 2020 presidential election. Thomas shares the different ways in which QAnon was able to almost completely overtake Twitter, one of the easiest mainstream social media platforms to share on, including an average of over 60,000 Q-related tweets and hashtags per day. The QAnon movement would get further legitimization through boosts from then president Trump, like when he tagged a QAnon account on Twitter while calling for harsher voter identification measures—an effort that is often seen as racially charged, since the people who have the most challenges toward voting access in the US tend to be people of color. Elise Thomas is a freelance writer whose work has appeared in Foreign Policy, *the Australian Broadcasting Corporation, the* Guardian, Wired UK, *and others.*

"Qanon Deploys 'Information Warfare' to Influence the 2020 Election," by Elise Thomas, *Wired*, February 17, 2020. Reprinted by permission.

As you read, consider the following questions:

1. How did the Russian interference into the 2016 US presidential election evolve into the information warfare seen online during the 2020 US presidential election?
2. What is the disparity between the number of QAnon adherents and their overall presence on social media?
3. Why are memes such an important tactic for QAnon adherents to spread their claims online?

When the notorious online forum 8chan was forced off the internet in August, after being linked to acts of violence including the Christchurch shooting, it looked like a blow to the Qanon conspiracy movement, which had made 8chan its virtual home. Rather than fade away, though, 8chan's Qanon posters migrated to other platforms, where they're still trying to use social media to influence elections.

The two most popular new homes for Qanon followers are Endchan and 8chan's successor 8kun. In late 2019, Qanon followers on Endchan used Twitter to influence governors' races in Kentucky and Louisiana, posting tweets and memes in favor of Republican candidates and attacking their opponents. They analyzed social media conversations, including popular hashtags, to decide where and how to weigh in. Both Republicans lost in close elections. Now, Qanon adherents are employing the same tactics on the 2020 presidential race.

"We need memes that are funny and mocking of the democrat candidates, but also that are informative and revealing about their policies that are WRONG for the United States of America and the American people," wrote a poster in a thread titled "Meme War 2020" on 8kun in November 2019. "We also need memes that are PRO-TRUMP, that explain how his policies are RIGHT for the United States of America and the American people, and that can debunk the smears and attacks that are no doubt going to come at POTUS again, and again."

Qanon followers have cultivated connections over social media with key Trump allies. President Trump himself has retweeted Qanon-linked accounts at least 72 times, including 20 times in one day in December 2019. Other influential Trump allies also promoted Qanon-linked accounts. For example, on December 23, Trump's personal lawyer Rudy Giuliani retweeted @QAnonWomen4Rudy (the bio of which reads "Patriotic Ladies supporting the sexiest man alive").

The Qanon conspiracy theory is based on the belief that Trump and a mysterious individual known as "Q" are battling against a powerful cabal of elite pedophiles in the media and Democratic Party. Q supposedly communicated with their followers through encoded posts known as "Q drops" on the quasi-anonymous forum 8chan. After 8chan was taken down, Q, or someone using the Q persona, resumed posting on 8kun.

Beginning early last year, Qanon followers more explicitly embraced concepts of "information warfare," efforts to shape narratives and people's beliefs to influence events. The Russian interference in the US elections in 2016 has been described as information warfare. In a February 2019 thread titled "Welcome to Information Warfare" on Endchan's Qanon research forum, a poster exhorted fellow users to "[g]et ready for a new phase in the battle anons: the fight to take back the narrative from the [mainstream media]." Now, Qanon users are trying to wield the same tactics to shape the political narrative for 2020.

On dedicated boards on Endchan and 8kun, Qanon posters monitor news and political content on Twitter. They build lists of hashtags to target, generate content and memes relating to the day's political developments, and share advice about how to create new social media accounts with plausible fake personas. The goal, broadly speaking, is to flood social media with pro-Trump, pro-Republican, and anti-Democrat narratives or, failing that, to simply hijack and derail conversations. Recent targets include Democratic members of the House of Representatives who voted to impeach

Trump, particularly those who represent districts that Trump carried in 2016.

"These democrats who were elected to congress in districts with patriots that voted for Trump are TRAITORS ... Part of the 2020 memewar NEEDS to be strategically targeting these now VERY VULNERABLE democrats with memes so that not only are they voted out of office but democrats lose the House," wrote a user on 8kun's Qanon board in December 2019. "Don't forget we are waging an information war, and this and the 2020 memewar are part of it."

The number of Qanon adherents is unknown but believed to be small. But Qanon followers wield outsize influence because of their presence on other social media, particularly Twitter. According to Marc-André Argentino, a PhD candidate at Concordia University, there were 22,232,285 tweets using #Qanon and related hashtags such as #Q, #Qpatriot, and #TheGreatAwakening in 2019—an average of 60,910 per day. The total exceeded other popular hashtags such as #MeToo (5,231,928 tweets in 2019) or #climatechange (7,510,311 tweets).

The movement also is important because of its influence on Trump and his allies. "I doubt that President Trump believes that there's someone in his inner circle leaking stories as 'Q-Clearance Patriot,'" says Ethan Zuckerman, Director of MIT's Center for Civic Media, who has previously written about the impact of Qanon on politics and society. "But anyone who's worked with Trump—in his business as well as presidential contexts—knows that Trump needs constant praise and soothing, and I suspect many Q-related memes make it to the president's attention as his aides try to stroke his ego."

"I don't see this as an intentional or instrumental relationship, but it's easy to see how it could benefit both sides," Zuckerman says.

The confluence of interests enables Qanon conspiracists to launder ideas into the mainstream in potentially dangerous ways. Like many other social movements born on the chan boards, the Qanon movement has had undertones of violence. Weeks after

Trump's 2016 election, a conspiracy believer armed with an AR-15 attacked a pizza restaurant in search of a pedophile ring he thought was being run from the basement. (The restaurant did not even have a basement.) The killing of a mob boss last year was linked to the alleged perpetrator's belief in Qanon, as were attempts to block the bridge next to Hoover Dam with an armored vehicle and to occupy a cement plant in Arizona. Internal documents reported last year show the FBI considers Qanon to be a domestic terrorism threat. The FBI said it does not confirm or deny the existence of an investigation.

The chan boards from which Qanon emerged have a long history of "raiding" behavior, in which users launch coordinated attacks on other online communities and platforms. In that context, it's not surprising that Qanon is active on social media ahead of the 2020 elections. What's surprising is the level of organization that the Endchan and 8kun Qanon subcommunities are demonstrating.

Last fall, Qanon conspiracists targeted the Louisiana and Kentucky gubernatorial elections by flooding key hashtags such as #vote and #VoteonNov5 with tweets and memes supporting the Republican candidates and smearing their opponents. Users following those hashtags could have been exposed to a torrent of pro-Republican, anti-Democrat content. Qanon adherents also sought to hijack pro-Democrat hashtags such as #VoteBlue and #JohnBelEdwards (the Democratic candidate in Louisiana) and troll Democrat accounts by replying to their tweets with comments and memes attacking the candidate.

On November 16, the day of Louisiana's runoff election, an Endchan user called on fellow posters to "raid" a Twitter thread by the Democratic Governors' Association in support of John Bel Edwards. Another user, calling out to "anons" (as users on the chan boards often call one another), posted memes criticizing Bel Edwards, claiming he "gives illegals your medical" and "allowed highest murder rate." (FBI statistics show Louisiana's murder rate rose in 2017 and fell in 2018 while Bel Edwards was governor.)

The meme was then posted on the Democratic Governors' Association's thread.

Memes are an important Qanon tactic, in part because, as images, they often evade efforts to moderate content. "Memes go around his censorship algorithms," a poster on the Qanon board on Endchan wrote in October. Qanon supporters stockpile hundreds of memes that followers can tap.

The members of the so-called Squad, four progressive Democratic congressmembers who are people of color, are particular targets. They are the subject of hundreds of memes stored on image-sharing accounts linked to the Qanon research boards. These memes often contain implicitly or overtly racist and sexist attacks, including monikers like "jihad squad" and "suicide squad."

There are also racial elements to Qanon's efforts to shift the ground on an important issue for 2020: voter identification.

Voter identification measures are controversial, because of concerns that they can unfairly discriminate against minority voters. The #voterid hashtag has been consistently targeted by Qanon over a period of months, including stockpiling hundreds of memes relating to voter ID and voter fraud in shared accounts on image-file-sharing sites.

Qanon followers employ multiple strategies to support voter ID laws, from accusing opponents of voter ID laws of racism, to leaning into Trump's own oft-repeated conspiracy theory that voter fraud favored the Democrats in 2016, to the confusing suggestion that a lack of voter ID laws helped Russian interference in the 2016 election. This willingness to shift narratives, testing out different means to the same end, echoes the way in which Russia's Internet Research Agency actively played on both sides of social media debates in 2016 in an effort to sow division.

In July 2019, Qanon's efforts on the #voterid hashtag got the biggest boost imaginable: Trump tagged the Qanon account @Voteridplease in a tweet calling for voter identification measures. His tweet was shared more than 140,000 times.

Julian Feeld, cohost of the Qanon Anonymous podcast, says Qanon is "a colorful expression of a broader and more worrying global trend towards 'information warfare' in the service of those seeking to consolidate capital and power." He says the group is "a harbinger of what's next for the American political discourse."

By promoting conspiracies and fomenting division, Zuckerman of the MIT Media Lab says, Qanon and similar movements threaten Americans' sense of shared truth. "The danger of Qanon is not that they try to blow up a building," he says. "It's that they and others are blowing up our shared reality."

"Over the past few months, big tech platforms like Facebook and Twitter have taken major steps toward deplatforming far-right extremists, leading them to gravitate to encrypted messaging apps like Telegram."

When One Door Closed, the QAnon Community Opened a Window

EJ Dickson

In the following viewpoint, EJ Dickson looks at the shift in QAnon conspiracy chatter in the online space following the successful swearing-in of President Joe Biden on January 20, 2021. According to the Center for Hate and Extremism, instead of the crisis of faith that it was assumed QAnon adherents would have following the discovery that none of Q's theories were actually factual, these people have shifted to the messaging app Telegram, which is currently serving as a bastion of far-right extremism. According to the author, there were actually increases in the channels used to follow QAnon conspiracy theories on inauguration day and the days surrounding it. EJ Dickson is a culture reporter for Rolling Stone.

As you read, consider the following questions:

1. Why would there be an increase in belief in the QAnon conspiracy following the 2021 inauguration of President Joe Biden, which invalidated most of Q's theories?
2. Why are platforms like Telegram, MeWe, Rumble, and Parler so popular with conspiracy theorists?
3. Per the viewpoint, are the QAnon adherents flocking to Telegram vulnerable to even further radicalization?

Now that the Biden administration is officially underway, the QAnon community is in crisis. Adherents to the conspiracy theory, which postulates the existence of a cabal of media and left-wing political figures engaged in a child trafficking ring, believed that Inauguration Day would serve as the Great Awakening, and that President Trump would swoop in and arrest and execute all of his enemies. Yet after Inauguration Day came and went without incident, many were left confused, disappointed, and disillusioned with the promises of Q.

As a result of the failed promise of an Inauguration Day reckoning, some extremism experts predicted that the community would be in turmoil, or that believers would undergo a crisis of faith and possibly turn away from the movement. On the encrypted messaging app Telegram, however, which is currently serving as a bastion of far-right extremism, the QAnon community is not just thriving, but growing, according to data from the Center for Hate and Extremism.

"QAnon data shows no mass exodus as some predicted and in fact, in some cases, there was increases in over a 24-hour cycle," says Kevin Grisham, the associate director of the Center for Hate and Extremism, which provided the data to *Rolling Stone*. Of the nine QAnon-related channels on the platform his team was tracking, eight experienced a boost in followers between January 20th, the day of Biden's inauguration, and January 21st. One channel in particular grew by more than 35 percent, from 16,695 followers to

22,851 (*Rolling Stone* is declining to cite the specific channels on the grounds that they feature disturbing and extremist content).

On social media, there has been some speculation that such growth can be attributed in part to an influx of journalists and federal law enforcement officers following the Capitol riots. Yet the content of the discourse on the groups, says Grisham, is noteworthy. Overwhelmingly, followers are "still hoping to 'hold the line' and the plan will happen," he says.

"Right now, I'm not sure that the reporting about [QAnon believers] snapping out of it is representative of the norm," says Jitarth Jadeja, a former QAnon believer based in Sydney, Australia. "I'm seeing a lot of doubling down, more than exits and questioning." Such doubling-down has taken many different forms, from believers arguing that Biden will be impeached to the prospect of a military coup to the idea that Biden is part of the "plan." Major influencers continue to echo the party line that Trump, Q, and his cohorts are still maintaining control behind the scenes, and that it is only a matter of time before the reckoning against the deep state takes place. "The storm has arrived. Stay safe and strong on the ground. Stay strong, stay calm, stay informed.... keep the faith, trust the plan," reads one post that was shared on multiple QAnon Telegram channels.

Over the past few months, big tech platforms like Facebook and Twitter have taken major steps toward deplatforming far-right extremists, leading them to gravitate to encrypted messaging apps like Telegram or smaller social networking apps with lax content moderation guidelines like MeWe or Rumble. The social networking app Parler, which markets itself as a free speech app, was also a popular choice for those on the right until it was removed from the Apple and Google Play stores earlier this month, following scrutiny over its role in helping to organize the January 6th Capitol riot. As a result of such deplatforming efforts, Telegram in particular has experienced a huge boost in its user base, with the app announcing it had increased by 25 million users in the days since Parler went dark.

As a result of those on the right who have been deplatformed flocking to apps like Telegram, there is a concern that members of fringe groups will feed off each other and the dangerous ideas they promote, creating cross-pollination of sorts. Such mixing of different types of far-right groups, as well as far-right and neo-Nazi groups actively calling on their members to try to convert QAnon believers in crisis, "could create some really dangerous situations," Grisham previously told *Rolling Stone*.

Researcher Marc-Andre Argentino of Concordia University echoes this concern. He has noticed similar growth in QAnon channels on Telegram, citing one channel with more than 131,000 followers that has grown steadily over the past 30 days. He attributes it in part to "Terrorgram" channels, or extremist groups on Telegram, "raiding QAnon channels post-inauguration in an attempt to recruit and radicalize QAnon adherents," he says.

Even without Trump in office, adherents clinging to the idea that Trump is still in power behind the scenes—or that Biden is secretly part of the "plan"—could pose a huge threat. "The true believers [could] be most dangerous," says Grisham.

"With Trump in office, he kept them calm, they thought everything was under control, that they didn't need to do anything, trust the plan and all that jazz," says Jadeja. "Now I think they'll start coming up with their own plans."

"As ThinkProgress reporter Luke Barnes aptly points out, part of the reason that the QAnon conspiracy theory has sustained growth for so long is that it exists as a big tent under which countless other theories have been folded."

The Mainstream Media Met QAnon at a Trump Rally

Jared Holt

In the following viewpoint, Jared Holt describes how the QAnon conspiracy met the mainstream media for one of the first times, at a rally that was held for President Trump's re-election in Tampa, Florida. The presence of QAnon adherents at the rally brought it out of the dark right-wing spaces and into the forefront. One example is when QAnon believers shouted at CNN's reporter Jim Acosta to ask Trump about Q. The author shares how one of the primary reasons the conspiracy resonates is because of how broad it is—from banking to Satanic abuse and alleged sex trafficking by Democratic lawmakers and other public figures. Jared Holt is an investigative reporter for People for the American Way, where he covers extremist movements in America.

"QAnon Meets the Mainstream at Tampa Trump Rally," by Jared Holt, Right Wing Watch, August 1, 2018. Reprinted by permission.

As you read, consider the following questions:

1. How was Pizzagate one of the earliest catalysts for the QAnon conspiracy theory in 2018, and then through the 2020 presidential election?
2. What are ways in which the QAnon conspiracy theory made it into the mainstream media prior to the Tampa rally?
3. How does a QAnon evangelist speaking at the Heritage Foundation further connect and legitimize the conspiracy to President Trump?

Mainstream press covering the White House got their first unignorably palpable taste of "The Storm" conspiracy theory and its anonymous protagonist, "QAnon," last night at President Trump's rally in Tampa, Florida.

The conspiracy theory—which supposes that President Trump is secretly undoing a global satanic pedophile ring with the help of Special Counsel Robert Mueller and ordering a top-level staffer to share information about the efforts via cryptic posts on the anonymous imageboard 8chan—currently captivates hundreds of thousands of right-wing activists online. Some spend hours per day in chat rooms dedicated to decoding the "crumbs" (clues) that an anonymous writer using the moniker "Q" posts online.

For mainstream media reporters, the presence of QAnon believers at the Tampa rally heralded a new phenomenon, but this conspiracy theory has been churning beneath the veneer of right-wing media for the better part of a year, and has occupied major space in right-wing internet watering holes.

The conspiracy theory has also bled into real life in various ways. In June, a man with a gun barricaded himself inside an armored vehicle on top of the Hoover Dam, demanding the release of what they believe to be a secret report that was made by the Justice Department's Office of Inspector General—a likely mythical document that QAnon followers have surmised will validate their conspiracy theories once and for all. More recently, lawyer Michael Avenatti, who is representing adult film actress Stephanie Clifford (a.k.a., Stormy Daniels) in a lawsuit against the president, faced in-person intimidation from a suspected QAnon supporter after Q targeted his office for harassment. In April, QAnon supporters marched in Washington.

Last month, the Trump campaign gave VIP access to a QAnon supporter. And an early evangelist of QAnon spoke at the Heritage Foundation, which is arguably the most powerful think tank in Washington for its role in staffing and policy-setting for the Trump administration. Earlier this year, longtime conservative organizations like Operation Rescue hopped aboard the conspiracy theory. Even Trump-supporting personalities purporting to be journalists have kept tabs on QAnon and made public winks toward the supporting base. If that weren't enough, the conspiracy theory was promoted by Tampa's own county GOP.

In Tampa, QAnon believers heckled reporters, including CNN's Jim Acosta. In a video uploaded to Twitter, one QAnon believer shouts at Acosta, "Ask Trump about Q! Ask Trump about Q!"

As ThinkProgress reporter Luke Barnes aptly points out, part of the reason that the QAnon conspiracy theory has sustained growth for so long is that it exists as a big tent under which countless other theories have been folded. Barnes writes:

> The expansive nature of the QAnon theory—it involves everything from banking conspiracies to claims of Satanic Abuse and supposed child sex trafficking by Democratic lawmakers and public figures—means that smaller theories can be adopted into the fold as offshoots. For example, over the last two months in Arizona, a group called Veterans on Patrol has been "investigating" what they claim is an abandoned "child sex camp" tied to QAnon, and have been harassing public officials who say that those claims are bogus.

Another aspect of the QAnon conspiracy theory that makes it so infectious to its adherents is the belief that their theories are being noticed and validated by the Trump administration.

Supporters have claimed that Trump is nodding to them by reciting snippets of slogans associated with the conspiracy theory, and have alleged that Trump is making hand gestures to signal to them.

Much like the "Pizzagate" conspiracies of years past, the QAnon conspiracy theory has become a surprisingly hearty side dish within pro-Trump media diets across the country, and plays to conspiracy theories about satanic pedophilia rings that have permeated in the American zeitgeist since the 1980s. It's one of many symptoms of the new reality that Trump and his accessories have successfully validated among his supporters—an alternate reality in which the news is "fake" and the "deep state" clique is out to sabotage American patriots.

Conspiracy theories have long been an American pastime, but one that most politicians have historically left to media personalities to peddle on their behalf. However, once the "birther" Trump was elected, one of those conspiracy theory hawks walked into the most powerful office in the free world and became the mouthpiece of America.

All of this is to say that the QAnon folks' pronounced presence in Tampa shouldn't have been so surprising. It's just the new reality.

Periodical and Internet Sources Bibliography

The following articles have been selected to supplement the diverse views presented in this chapter.

Jack Brewster, "QAnon Content Is 'Evaporating' from the Internet, New Report Finds," *Forbes*, May 26, 2021. https://www.forbes.com/sites/jackbrewster/2021/05/26/qanon-content-is-evaporating-from-the-internet-new-report-finds/?sh=248c255012b7

Jack Brewster, "'Q' Hasn't Posted in Six Months—But Some QAnon Followers Still Keep The Faith," *Forbes*, June 8, 2021. https://www.forbes.com/sites/jackbrewster/2021/06/08/q-hasnt-posted-in-6-months-but-some-qanon-followers-still-keep-the-faith/?sh=37c14ed60717

Dani Di Placido, "HBO's 'Q: Into the Storm' Exposes the Strange Truth Behind the QAnon Delusion," *Forbes*, April 13, 2021. https://www.forbes.com/sites/danidiplacido/2021/04/13/hbos-q-into-the-storm-exposes-the-strange-truth-behind-the-qanon-delusion/?sh=7eecfdb26ba3

France 24 Staff, "Swiss Text Sleuths Unpick Mystery of QAnon Origins," France 24, January 17, 2021. https://www.france24.com/en/live-news/20210117-swiss-text-sleuths-unpick-mystery-of-qanon-origins

Rachel E. Greenspan, "The History of QAnon: How the Conspiracy Theory Snowballed from the Fringes of the Internet into the Mainstream," *Insider*, February 11, 2021. https://www.insider.com/qanon-history-who-is-q-conspiracy-theory-what-does-believe-2021-2

Andrew Griffin, "What Is QAnon? The Origins of Bizarre Conspiracy Theory Spreading Online," *The Independent*, January 21, 2021. https://www.independent.co.uk/life-style/gadgets-and-tech/news/what-is-qanon-b1790868.html

Matthew Hannah, "QAnon and the Information Dark Age," First Monday, 2020. https://firstmonday.org/ojs/index.php/fm/article/view/10868/10067

Tyler Hersko, "'Q: Into the Storm' Review: HBO Gives Conspiracy Theorists a Puff Piece," *Indiewire*, March 21, 2021. https://www.indiewire.com/2021/03/q-into-the-storm-hbo-documentary-review-1234624486/

Adrienne LaFrance, "The Prophecies of Q," *The Atlantic*, June 2020. https://www.theatlantic.com/magazine/archive/2020/06/qanon-nothing-can-stop-what-is-coming/610567/

Marisa Meltzer, "QAnon's Unexpected Roots in New Age Spirituality," *Washington Post*, March 29, 2021. https://www.washingtonpost.com/magazine/2021/03/29/qanon-new-age-spirituality/

Giovanni Russonello, "QAnon Now as Popular in US as Some Major Religions, Poll Suggests," *New York Times*, May 27, 2021. https://www.nytimes.com/2021/05/27/us/politics/qanon-republicans-trump.html

Mike Wendling, "QAnon: What Is It and Where Did It Come From?" BBC News, January 6, 2021. https://www.bbc.com/news/53498434

Brandy Zadrozny and Ben Collins, "How Three Conspiracy Theorists Took 'Q' and Sparked Qanon," NBC News, August 14, 2018. https://www.nbcnews.com/tech/tech-news/how-three-conspiracy-theorists-took-q-sparked-qanon-n900531

What Are the Dangers of Legitimizing QAnon and Similar Conspiracy Theories in the Mainstream Media?

Chapter Preface

While social media platforms like Facebook and Twitter have grown more and more prevalent as places where people get their news online, mainstream and more traditional journalistic platforms still maintain the most viewership, following, and trust with people in the United States. But what happens when these mainstream organizations lend legitimacy to a baseless and unfounded conspiracy theory like QAnon?

What impact does it have on a conspiracy theory to invite its believers to speak on television in front of millions of viewers, including those who for whatever reason are more susceptible to believing in these conspiracies? What impact does a news organization have when taking something that is unable to be proven because it is so broad and treat it as seriously as it would a presidential debate? What impact does a social media platform have when it does not take down inaccurate information, just because an account with a significant number of followers—in the tens of millions—says it is true?

Such legitimization has led to the election of QAnon self-professed "true believers" like Marjorie Taylor Greene of Georgia to the US Congress. It also had a hand in the US Capitol insurrection on January 6, 2021. Facebook and Twitter finally banned former president Trump after the riot, but why did it take such a dramatic event for them to take action, when it could be argued that Trump's rhetoric and legitimization of QAnon were already a clear and present danger to American society for months leading up to the riot?

And what happens when a conspiracy theory like QAnon decides to take on the task of spreading misinformation on something that would impact the health—the lives—of all people in the US and the world, the COVID-19 pandemic?

The viewpoints in the following chapter explore how the legitimization of QAnon in the mainstream media allowed the conspiracy to gain a foothold within American society that it is still attempting to grapple with.

> *"While there's no silver bullet for online misinformation and extremist content, there's also no doubt platforms could have done more in the past that may have prevented the scenes witnessed in Washington DC."*

Social Media Giants Took Too Long to Confront Trump's Lies

Timothy Graham

In the following viewpoint, Timothy Graham chronicles the fallout from the January 6 insurrection at the US Capitol, including Facebook and Twitter banning former president Donald Trump from the platform, citing "risk of further incitement of violence." Among the content to be taken down prior to the banning of his accounts was a video in which Trump told the insurrectionists at the Capitol to go home and followed up with telling them that they were "very special" and that he loved them for disruption of Congress's certification of President Joe Biden's win in November 2020. Timothy Graham is senior lecturer at Queensland University of Technology in Australia whose research combines computational methods with social theory to study online networks and platforms, with a particular interest in online bots and trolls and disinformation.

"Social Media Giants Finally Confronted Trump's Lies. But Why Wait Until There Was a Riot in the Capitol?" by Timothy Graham, The Conversation, January 7, 2021, https://theconversation.com/social-media-giants-have-finally-confronted-trumps-lies-but-why-wait-until-there-was-a-riot-in-the-capitol-152820.

As you read, consider the following questions:

1. When would have been a better time to enact the social media bans?
2. Should Trump have been allowed to maintain his personal accounts, with certain content removed?
3. Does the banning of Trump and similar conspiracy-based accounts on Twitter help or hurt attempts to stem misinformation online?

After the chaos in the US Capitol, stoked largely by rhetoric from President Donald Trump, Twitter has permanently suspended his account, which had 88.7 million followers, citing "risk of further incitement of violence."

Facebook and Instagram had earlier locked Trump's accounts—with 35.2 million followers and 24.5 million, respectively—for at least two weeks, the remainder of his presidency. This ban was extended from 24 hours.

The locks are the latest effort by social media platforms to clamp down on Trump's misinformation and baseless claims of election fraud.

They came after Twitter labelled a video posted by Trump and said it posed a "risk of violence." Twitter removed users' ability to retweet, like or comment on the post—the first time this has been done.

In the video, Trump told the agitators at the Capitol to go home, but at the same time called them "very special" and said he loved them for disrupting the Congressional certification of President-elect Joe Biden's win.

That tweet has since been taken down for "repeated and severe violations" of Twitter's civic integrity policy. YouTube and Facebook have also removed copies of the video.

But as people across the world scramble to make sense of what's going on, one thing stands out: the events that transpired today were not unexpected.

Too Little Too Late?

Since the conspiracy's rise in 2017, it has always been unclear just how many Trump supporters buy into it—even as the QAnon presence at the president's rallies continues to grow dramatically. (During a Trump rally last year, an opening speaker recited the QAnon motto onstage.) But according to NBC News, a recent internal investigation conducted by Facebook has produced some rough data on the movement's size, as it connected millions of the site's users to massive QAnon groups and pages. The evaluation's initial results identified that more than 1 million accounts are members of 10 notable QAnon Facebook groups, a feature that allows users with shared interests to create public or private spaces to interact and organize. Although the percentage of overlap between the groups is unknown, the investigation also looked into users who joined similar groups and pages, resulting in the total number of QAnon affiliated accounts surpassing 3 million.

Facebook will reportedly look at the results of the investigation to determine whether or not the site's already massive population of QAnon supporters will be allowed to continue organizing unfettered. Last week, Facebook did ban a public QAnon group that had nearly 200,000 members, which was reportedly one of the largest such communities on the site. A spokesperson for the site told Reuters that the company is actively monitoring similar groups. In the spring, numerous other QAnon groups and pages on Facebook were permanently shut down due to "coordinated inauthentic behavior," the site said.

QAnon followers don't just use Facebook to build up massive virtual communities, as these online interactions are bleeding out into the real world. Facebook recently found $12,000 worth of ads, according to NBC News, "praising, supporting, or representing" QAnon that have run on the site, including one ad—of 185 total—aimed at organizing a "QAnon March for Children" in Detroit.

Facebook asserts that the platform consistently takes "action against accounts, Groups, and Pages tied to QAnon that break our rules," stated a spokesperson, who requested anonymity in NBC's report due to concerns that QAnon followers would retaliate against them personally. "We have teams assessing our policies against QAnon and are currently exploring additional actions we can take."

"Is Social Media's QAnon Crackdown Too Late?" by Caleb Ecarma, *Vanity Fair*, August 11, 2020.

Given the lack of regulation and responsibility shown by platforms over the past few years, it's fair to say the writing was on the wall.

The Real, Violent Consequences of Misinformation

While Trump is no stranger to contentious and even racist remarks on social media, Twitter's action to lock the president's account is a first.

The line was arguably crossed by Trump's implicit incitement of violence and disorder within the halls of the US Capitol itself.

Nevertheless, it would have been a difficult decision for Twitter (and Facebook and Instagram), with several factors at play. Some of these are short-term, such as the immediate potential for further violence.

Then there's the question of whether tighter regulation could further incite rioting Trump supporters, by feeding into their theories claiming there's a large-scale "deep state" plot against the president. It's possible.

But a longer-term consideration—and perhaps one at the forefront of the platforms' priorities—is how these actions will affect their value as commercial assets.

I believe the platforms' biggest concern is their own bottom line. They are commercial companies legally obliged to pursue profits for shareholders. Commercial imperatives and user engagement are at the forefront of their decisions.

What happens when you censor a Republican president? You can lose a huge chunk of your conservative user base, or upset your shareholders.

Despite what we think of them, or how we might use them, platforms such as Facebook, Twitter, Instagram and YouTube aren't set up in the public interest.

For them, it's risky to censor a head of state when they know that content is profitable. Doing it anyway involves a complex risk calculus—with priorities being the shareholders, the companies' market value and their reputation.

Walking a Tightrope

The platforms' decisions to not only force the removal of several of Trump's posts, but also to lock his accounts, carries enormous potential loss of revenue. It's a major and irreversible step.

They are now forced to keep a close eye on one another. If one appears too "strict" in its censorship, it may attract criticism, lose user engagement and ultimately profit. At the same time, if platforms are too loose with their content regulation, they must weather the storm of public critique.

You don't want to be the last organisation to make the tough decision, but you don't necessarily want to be the first, either—because then you're the "trial balloon" who volunteered to potentially harm the bottom line.

For all major platforms, the past few years have presented high stakes. Yet there have been plenty of opportunities to stop the situation snowballing to where it is now.

From Trump's baseless election fraud claims to his false ideas about the coronavirus, time and again platforms have turned a blind eye to serious cases of mis- and disinformation.

The storming of the Capitol is a logical consequence of this and has arguably been a long time coming.

During the coronavirus pandemic, while Trump was partially censored by Twitter and Facebook for misinformation, the platforms failed to take lasting action to deal with the issue at its core.

In the past, platforms have cited constitutional reasons to justify not censoring politicians. They have claimed a civic duty to give elected officials an unfiltered voice.

This line of argument should have ended with the "Unite the Right" rally in Charlottesville, in August 2017, when Trump responded to the killing of an anti-fascism protester by claiming there were "very fine people on both sides."

An Age of QAnon, Proud Boys and Neo-Nazis

While there's no silver bullet for online misinformation and extremist content, there's also no doubt platforms could have done more in the past that may have prevented the scenes witnessed in Washington DC.

In a crisis, there's a rush to make sense of everything. But we need only look at what led us to this point. Experts on disinformation have been crying out for platforms to do more to combat disinformation and its growing domestic roots.

Now, in 2021, extremists such as neo-Nazis and QAnon believers no longer have to lurk in the depths of online forums or commit lone acts of violence. Instead, they can violently storm the Capitol.

It would be a cardinal error to not appraise the severity of the neglect that led us here. In some ways, perhaps that's the biggest lesson we can learn.

> *"Tweets written in English had a high level of antisemitism. In particular, they targeted public figures such as Jewish-American billionaire investor and philunthropist George Soros, or revived old conspiracies about secret Jewish plots for world domination."*

Trump's Twitter Legacy Lives On in the Global Spread of QAnon Conspiracy Theories

Verica Rupar and Tom De Smedt

In the following viewpoint, Verica Rupar and Tom De Smedt share the overall impact former president Donald Trump had and still has on social media in spite of his banning and the mainstream social media platforms' attempts to remove misinformation based on the election online. Being permitted to utilize his social media, specifically Twitter, mostly unchecked during his four years as president enabled QAnon, its conspiracy theory, and other conspiracies with connections to radicalized antisemitic rhetoric to spread unchecked on the platform and on social media in general, especially with a following of 88 million users at the time his account was banned in January 2021 following the insurrection at the US Capitol. Verica Rupar is a professor at Auckland University of Technology. Tom De Smedt is a postdoctoral research associate at the University of Antwerp.

"Trump's Time Is Up, but His Twitter Legacy Lives On in the Global Spread of Qanon Conspiracy Theories," by Verica Rupar and Tom De Smedt, The Conversation, January 19, 2021, https://theconversation.com/trumps-time-is-up-but-his-twitter-legacy-lives-on-in-the-global-spread-of-qanon-conspiracy-theories-153298.

As you read, consider the following questions:

1. What are the main topics identified in the viewpoint to spread the most QAnon content online?
2. What is the connection between the toxicity in QAnon-based tweets and anti-Semitic rhetoric?
3. What more can be done to stop the spread of misinformation online, according to the authors?

"The lie outlasts the liar," writes historian Timothy Snyder, referring to outgoing president Donald Trump and his contribution to the "post-truth" era in the US.

Indeed, the mass rejection of reason that erupted in a political mob storming Capitol Hill mere weeks before the inauguration of Joe Biden tests our ability to comprehend contemporary American politics and its emerging forms of extremism.

Much has been written about Trump's role in spreading misinformation and the media failures that enabled him. His contribution to fuelling extremism, flirting with the political fringe, supporting conspiracy theories and, most of all, Twitter demagogy created an environment in which he has been seen as an "accelerant" in his own right.

If the scale of international damage is yet to be calculated, there is something we can measure right now.

In September last year, the London-based Media Diversity Institute (MDI) asked us to design a research project that would systematically track the extent to which US-originated conspiracy theory group QAnon had spread to Europe.

Titled QAnon 2: Spreading Conspiracy Theories on Twitter, the research is part of the international Get the Trolls Out! (GTTO) project, focusing on religious discrimination and intolerance.

Twitter and the Rise of QAnon

GTTO media monitors had earlier noted the rise of QAnon support among Twitter users in Europe and were expecting a further surge of derogatory talk ahead of the 2020 US presidential election.

We examined the role religion played in spreading conspiracy theories, the most common topics of tweets, and what social groups were most active in spreading QAnon ideas.

We focused on Twitter because its increasing use—some sources estimate 330 million people used Twitter monthly in 2020—has made it a powerful political communication tool. It has given politicians such as Trump the opportunity to promote, facilitate and mobilise social groups on an unprecedented scale.

Using AI tools developed by data company Textgain, we analysed about half-a-million Twitter messages related to QAnon to identify major trends.

By observing how hashtags were combined in messages, we examined the network structure of QAnon users posting in English, German, French, Dutch, Italian and Spanish. Researchers identified about 3,000 different hashtags related to QAnon used by 1,250 Twitter profiles.

An American Export

Every fourth QAnon tweet originated in the US (300). Far behind were tweets from other countries: Canada (30), Germany (25), Australia (20), the United Kingdom (20), the Netherlands (15), France (15), Italy (10), Spain (10) and others.

We examined QAnon profiles that share each other's content, Trump tweets and YouTube videos, and found over 90% of these profiles shared the content of at least one other identified profile.

Seven main topics were identified: support for Trump, support for EU-based nationalism, support for QAnon, deep state conspiracies, coronavirus conspiracies, religious conspiracies and political extremism.

Hashtags rooted in US evangelicalism sometimes portrayed Trump as Jesus, as a superhero, or clad in medieval armour, with

Conspiracy Theories Go Viral

Online conspiracy theories are surprisingly convincing—and present significant danger to the real world. At Jigsaw, a division of Google focused on countering digital extremism, cyberattacks and misinformation, we conducted more than 70 in-depth interviews in 2020 with people in the US and UK who believe the Earth is flat, that school shootings were government plots and that white populations are being intentionally replaced by non-whites.

Those beliefs lead to changes in behaviour: we found that people who believe disinformation about the origin of Covid-19 shun face masks and ignore social-distancing. In 2021, anti-vaccination activists will use the internet to warn about what they see as nefarious motives behind any pandemic-vaccination programme.

Social-media platforms have now started to respond to Covid-related, racist and xenophobic conspiracy theories by removing content associated with these from their sites. This will protect unsuspecting people from stumbling across them. But the propaganda itself will not disappear. In 2021, these ideas will resurface on "alt-tech" networks such as Gab, Telegram and 8kun, platforms that market themselves as being "anti-censorship" (read: unmoderated) and for "free speech" (read: hate speech welcome). For the first time since the dawn of the social-media age, online content will go viral elsewhere.

underlying Biblical references to a coming apocalypse in which he will defeat the forces of evil.

Overall, the coronavirus pandemic appears to function as an important conduit for all such messaging, with QAnon acting as a rallying flag for discontent among far-right European movements.

Measuring the Toxicity of Tweets

We used Textgain's hate-speech detection tools to assess toxicity. Tweets written in English had a high level of antisemitism. In particular, they targeted public figures such as Jewish-American billionaire investor and philanthropist George Soros, or revived old conspiracies about secret Jewish plots for world domination. Soros was also a popular target in other languages.

Moving dangerous content into the "alt-tech" world will present two dangers. The first is that the inaccessibility of these subjects could encourage people to seek them out. Spreaders of conspiracy theories will have the opportunity to sensationalise a "censored" video ("what they don't want you to see")—what is known in online marketing as a "curiosity gap."

The second is that, ironically, the displacement of those ideas to more fringe platforms could help them spread, removing scepticism they may face from mainstream audiences.

Our interviews with hardcore conspiracists revealed the need to signal in-group status by voicing agreement and even engaging in one-upmanship by expanding on the conspiracy.

In 2021, we may feel reassured that social media companies are taking on a limited role as moderators. However, it is likely that the narratives with the greatest potential to cause harm will thrive away from the major platforms and, similar to QAnon in the US, find alternative routes into mainstream consciousness. Just because we can't see them, won't mean that they don't continue to pose a threat.

"Conspiracy Theories Are About to Go Viral in New, Murkier Ways," by Yasmin Green, *Wired*, January 9, 2021.

We also found a highly polarised debate around the coronavirus public health measures employed in Germany, often using Third Reich rhetoric.

New language to express negative sentiments was coined and then adopted by others—in particular, pejorative terms for face masks and slurs directed at political leaders and others who wore masks.

Accompanying memes ridiculed political leaders, displaying them as alien reptilian overlords or antagonists from popular movies, such as Star Wars Sith Lords and the cyborg from *The Terminator*.

Most of the QAnon profiles tap into the same sources of information: Trump tweets, YouTube disinformation videos and each other's tweets. It forms a mutually reinforcing confirmation bias—the tendency to search for, interpret, favour, and recall information that confirms prior beliefs or values.

Where Does It End?

Harvesting discontent has always been a powerful political tool. In a digital world this is more true than ever.

By mid 2020, Donald Trump had six times more followers on Twitter than when he was elected. Until he was suspended from the platform, his daily barrage of tweets found a ready audience in ultra-right groups in the US who helped his misinformation and inflammatory rhetoric jump the Atlantic to Europe.

Social media platforms have since attempted to reduce the spread of QAnon. In July 2020, Twitter suspended 7,000 QAnon-related accounts. In August, Facebook deleted over 790 groups and restricted the accounts of hundreds of others, along with thousands of Instagram accounts.

In January this year, all Trump's social media accounts were either banned or restricted. Twitter suspended 70,000 accounts that share QAnon content at scale.

But further Textgain analysis of 50,000 QAnon tweets posted in December and January showed toxicity had almost doubled, including 750 tweets inciting political violence and 500 inciting violence against Jewish people.

Those tweets were being systematically removed by Twitter. But calls for violence ahead of the January 20 inauguration continued to proliferate, Trump's QAnon supporters appearing as committed and vocal as ever.

The challenge for both the Biden administration and the social media platforms themselves is clear. But our analysis suggests any solution will require a coordinated international effort.

Viewpoint 

> *"Whoever Q is, the account has pretty much stopped posting on those message boards since the 2020 election."*

The Capitol Riots Underscore How QAnon Has Leaped from the Fringes of the Internet to the Real World

Shannon Bond

In the following viewpoint, Shannon Bond argues that social media platforms like Facebook, Twitter, and Instagram finally got aggressive on cracking down on accounts promoting QAnon after the January 6 attack on the US Capitol. The risk of QAnon adherents moving to fringe sites like Telegram and Gab is that they are able to share their theories and alleged evidence in unmoderated spaces, and also that these are places that are rife for further and more dangerous radicalization and encouragement of extremist behavior. Shannon Bond is a business correspondent at NPR who covers technology and how Silicon Valley's biggest companies are transforming how we live, work, and communicate.

As you read, consider the following questions:

1. What are the dangers of QAnon adherents moving into fringe sites following the banning on mainstream social media platforms?
2. What are the benefits to QAnon no longer having access to mainstream platforms like Twitter and Facebook?
3. Is it possible to completely remove QAnon conspiracy and other conspiracy theories from the online space?

January brought a one-two punch that should have knocked out the fantastical, false QAnon conspiracy theory.

After the Jan. 6 attack on the US Capitol, the social media platforms that had long allowed the falsehoods to spread like wildfire—namely Twitter, Facebook and YouTube—got more aggressive in cracking down on accounts promoting QAnon.

Just two weeks later, Joe Biden was inaugurated president. That stunned those adherents who believed, among other things, that Donald Trump would stay in office for another term and that he would arrest and execute his political enemies.

"There's no one cohesive narrative that's really emerged yet. And I pin that on [QAnon] not really having a leader right now," said Mike Rothschild, a conspiracy theory researcher who is writing a book about QAnon.

The QAnon universe has two stars. There's Q, the mysterious figure whose cryptic, evidence-free posts on anonymous online message boards spawned the baseless claim that a satanic cabal of pedophiles runs rampant in government and Hollywood. The other star is Trump, who was supposed to expose and defeat that cabal.

But both figures have gone silent online. Whoever Q is, the account has pretty much stopped posting on those message boards since the 2020 election. Trump was kicked off Facebook, Twitter and Google's YouTube after urging his supporters to go to the Capitol.

And yet, even as the big social media platforms try to squash harmful misinformation and hate speech, the conspiracy has survived in the darker corners of the Internet. As QAnon believers splinter onto different fringe platforms, experts warn they could absorb even more dangerous conspiracy theories and ideologies. What's more, QAnon has gained defenders in conservative media and among Republicans in Congress.

The events of Jan. 6 underscore how QAnon has leaped from the fringes of the Internet to the real world. Some rioters in the pro-Trump mob that stormed the Capitol openly expressed support for QAnon. That prompted Twitter, which along with Facebook and YouTube had started limiting QAnon content last year, to clamp down even more.

In the days after the Capitol insurrection, Twitter banned 70,000 QAnon-linked accounts for spreading the conspiracy theory. Some belonged to influencers with large followings, including high-profile Trump supporters Sidney Powell and Michael Flynn, who had also spread false claims of election fraud and had tried to get the election results overturned.

The result? "There isn't one central place that people are finding information in terms of influential accounts, and it's kind of become more disparate," said Melanie Smith of the research firm Graphika.

Graphika found that among a dense network of 14,000 QAnon-promoting Twitter accounts it has been tracking, 60% are now inactive. That splintering makes it harder for harmful, even violent ideas to gain traction—and less likely that unsuspecting Twitter users will stumble across them.

"For me, [this] is about not exposing new communities to that type of content," Smith said. "So in my mind, that's a pretty big success."

It's hard to quantify just how many people follow QAnon. When NPR and Ipsos polled people about whether they believe QAnon's core false claim—that "a group of Satan-worshipping elites who run a child sex ring are trying to control our politics and media"—17% said it was true, and another 37% said they didn't know.

While some people who may be susceptible to believing the falsehoods may never see them, Smith and other researchers warn there is a cost to that success: As QAnon influencers and their followers are pushed off mainstream platforms, some are migrating to apps with fewer rules, like the alternative social network Gab and the messaging app Telegram. There, they may be exposed to more extremist content, like that of white supremacist and neo-Nazi groups.

"What they're essentially doing is walking straight into an incubator for radicalization," said Jared Holt, a visiting research fellow at the Atlantic Council's Digital Forensic Research Lab, where he studies disinformation and extremism.

QAnon is already incorporating new, unfounded theories from other extremists. Some accounts are latching onto obscure legal fictions promoted by sovereign-citizen groups, which deny the legitimacy of the US government, such as the bogus idea that Trump will be inaugurated on March 4.

Holt said such adoption is "just another example of something that QAnon has done repeatedly, if not constantly, which is crowdsourcing their idea of reality."

QAnon's constant evolution presents a challenge for platforms like Twitter and Facebook in enforcing their bans by stamping out new conspiracy theories and hashtags appropriated by QAnon believers.

But even if effective, the platforms' actions can go only so far.

QAnon podcasts are available through Apple and Google. Fox News host Tucker Carlson recently defended QAnon adherents. QAnon has even gained a foothold in the halls of Congress, where two Republican members have openly supported some of the movement's baseless ideas.

"When you've got people like Tucker Carlson or sitting members of the House of Representatives talking about something, it's hard to ban it," said Rothschild, the researcher.

"I think this movement is now so mainstream and has pulled in so many people that it seems inconceivable that it will go away completely," he said.

> *"Although there is no scientific proof, the technology is suggested to negatively affect health on certain social media channels."*

The Conspiracy Theory Connecting COVID to 5G Spread Quickly Thanks to Twitter

Wasim Ahmed, Josep Vidal-Alaball, Joseph Downing, and López Seguí

In the following viewpoint, an excerpt from a research study, Wasim Ahmed, Josep Vidal-Alaball, Joseph Downing, and López Seguí explore the potential connection between 5G—the current technology standard for broadband cellular networks—and the COVID-19 conspiracy theory, one of the many conspiracy theories spread throughout 2020 since the pandemic reached the United States. The COVID-19 conspiracy theory is intrinsically connected to the QAnon conspiracy theory, as former president Trump, who is either considered a believer in QAnon or someone who refused to denounce it, avoided disclosing the true dangers of COVID-19 as it made its way into the United States.

"COVID-19 and the 5G Conspiracy Theory: Social Network Analysis of Twitter Data," by Wasim Ahmed, Josep Vidal-Alaball, Joseph Downing, and López Seguí, *Journal of Medical Internet Research*, May 2020.

As you read, consider the following questions:

1. Though Twitter is a place where people can get real-time information and analysis, what happens if inaccurate information is spread at the same rapid pace?
2. What are three similarities and differences between the spread of false information about the QAnon conspiracy and misinformation about the COVID-19 pandemic?
3. Why would people believe that there is a link between the spread of COVID-19 and 5G cellular networks?

The coronavirus strains have been known since 1960 and usually cause up to 15% of common colds in humans each year, mainly in mild forms. Previously two variants of coronavirus have caused severe illnesses: severe acute respiratory syndrome (SARS) in 2002, with severe acute respiratory distress, resulting in 9.6% mortality; and Middle East respiratory syndrome in 2012, with a higher mortality rate of 34.4%.[1-3] The novel coronavirus (SARS coronavirus 2), the seventh coronavirus known to infect humans, is a positive single-stranded RNA virus that probably originated in a seafood market in Wuhan in December 2019.[4, 5] Since then, the coronavirus disease (COVID-19), named by the World Health Organization, has affected more than 2 million people worldwide, killing more than 130,000 of them.[6] The COVID-19 pandemic coincided with the launch and development of the 5G mobile network.

Compared to the current 4G networks, 5G wireless communications provide high data rates (ie, gigabytes per second), have low latency, and increase base station capacity and perceived quality of service.[7] The popularity of this technology arose because of the burst in smart electronic devices and wireless multimedia demand, which created a burden on existing networks. A key benefit of 5G is that some of the current issues with cellular networks such as poor data rates, capacity, quality of service, and latency will be solved.[7] Although there is no scientific proof, the technology is suggested to negatively affect health on certain social media channels.[8]

In the first week of January, some social media users pointed to 5G as being the cause of COVID-19 or accelerating its spread. The issue became a trending topic and appeared visible to all users on Twitter within the United Kingdom. Since then, multiple videos and news articles have been shared across social media linking the two together. The conspiracy has been of such a serious nature that, in Birmingham and Merseyside, United Kingdom, 5G masts were torched over concerns associating this technology and the spread of the disease, according to the British Broadcasting Corporation.[9] More concerningly, Nightingale hospital in Birmingham, United Kingdom, had its phone mast set on fire.[10] This is unwelcome damage especially at a time when hospitals are required to operate with maximum efficiency.

The independent fact-checking website Full Fact noted that the conspiracy was not true and concluded that the theories given to support the 5G claims were flawed.[11] The National Health Service Director, Stephen Powis, noted in a press conference that the 5G infrastructure is vital for the wider general population who are being asked to remain at home. He noted that: "I'm absolutely outraged and disgusted that people would be taking action against the infrastructure we need to tackle this emergency."[10]

The origin of this theory demonstrates the transnational dimension to the new media landscape and the way that fake news and conspiracy theories travel. Previous research has traced the emergence of the conspiracy theory to comments made by a Belgian doctor in January 2020, linking health concerns about 5G to the emergence of the coronavirus.[12] From April 2-6, 2020, it is estimated that at least 20 mobile phone masts were vandalized in the United Kingdom alone.[13] Social media is an important information source for a subset of the population, and previous seminal research has noted the potential of Twitter for providing real time content analysis, allowing public health authorities to rapidly respond to concerns raised by the public.[14] During the unfolding COVID-19 pandemic, recent research has found that platforms such as YouTube have immense reach and can be used to educate the public.[15] Furthermore, recent research has also called for more understanding of public reactions on social media platforms related to COVID-19.[15]

The aim of this study was to analyze the 5G and COVID-19 conspiracy theory. More specifically, the research objectives were to answer the following questions: (1) who is spreading this conspiracy theory on Twitter; (2) what online sources of information are people referring to; (3) do people on Twitter really believe 5G and COVID-19 are linked; and (4) what steps and actions can public health authorities take to mitigate the spread of this conspiracy theory?

[...]

Discussion

Academics have been alarmed at the rate of fake news and misinformation across social media.[28-32] Initially, social media platforms had been praised for their ability to spread liberal messages during events such as the Arab Spring[22] and during the initial launch of WikiLeaks.[33] False information has been a genuine concern among social media platforms during COVID-19, and Facebook has implemented a new feature that will inform users if they have engaged with false information.[34]

One method of counteracting fake news is to be able to detect it rapidly and address it head-on at the time that it occurs. In the specific influencer analysis, there was a lack of an authority figure who was actively combating such misinformation. This study found that a dedicated individual Twitter account set up to spread the conspiracy theory formed a cluster in the network with 408 other Twitter users. This account, at the time of analysis, had managed to send a total of 303 tweets during this specific time period before it was closed down by Twitter. In hindsight, if this account would have been closed down much sooner, this would have halted the spread of this specific conspiracy theory. Moreover, if other users who were sharing humorous content and link baiting the hashtag refrained from tweeting about the topic and instead reported conspiracy-related tweets to Twitter, the hashtag would not have reached trending status on Twitter. As more users began to tweet using the hashtag, the overall visibility increased. Public health authorities may wish to advise citizens against resharing or engaging with misinformation on social media and encourage users to flag them as inappropriate to the social media companies. Many social media platforms provide users with the ability to report inappropriate content.

A further method of counteracting misinformation is to seek the assistance of influential public authorities and bodies such as public figures, government accounts, relevant scientific experts, doctors, or journalists. A further key point to make is that the fight against misinformation should take place on the platform where it arises. This is because people will not go to a website to read the counteracting report, but they will watch a video or a memo voice sent via WhatsApp or posted on a social media platform. Public TV, newspapers, and radio stations could also seek to devote regular programs to counteract fake news by discussing conspiracy theories that were spreading at the time. It could also be argued that it is important to analyze the context of the fake news and why it is spreading. Are people afraid? Does the theory propose a risk? Any content that aims to correct misinformation should aim to dispel people's fears.

This research set out to address four research questions that are now discussed. In regard to identifying how the conspiracy was spreading on Twitter, this article shows that a number of citizens who believed the conspiracy theory were actively tweeting and spreading it. A dedicated account that was set up for the sole purpose of spreading the conspiracy theory was identified. We also identified the "humor effect" in the sense that even those users who joined the discussion to mock the conspiracy theory inadvertently drew more attention to it.

In addressing the second research objective, this paper identifies a number of influential online sources that created content aiming to show a link between COVID-19 and 5G. These consisted of the website InfoWars, a commercial organization selling products that protect against electromagnetic fields. A website dedicated to linking 5G to COVID-19 was also identified. Specific YouTube videos and the YouTube domain itself were also found to be influential.

The third research objective was to identify whether people really believed 5G and COVID-19 were linked, as Twitter is known to contain humorous content.[16] It was found that 34.8% (n=81/233) of individual tweets contained views that 5G and COVID-19 were linked. Although it is a low percentage, there are indeed users who genuinely believe COVID-19 and 5G are linked.

In regard to the fourth research objective, this article sought to identify and discuss potential actions public health authorities could take to mitigate the spread of the conspiracy theory. Specifically, this study found that an individual account had been set up to spread the conspiracy theory and was able to attract a following and send out many tweets. Based on our analysis of this conspiracy theory on Twitter, its spread could have been halted if the accounts set up to spread misinformation were taken down faster than they were. Public health authorities should also aim to focus on these types of accounts in combating misinformation during the current COVID-19 pandemic. In addition, an authority figure with a sizeable following could have tweeted messages against the conspiracy theory and urged other users that the best way to deal with it is to not comment on, retweet, or link bait using the hashtag. This is because when users joined the discussion to dispel, ridicule, or piggyback on the hashtag, the topic was raised to new heights and had increased visibility.

A strength of this study is that it has identified the drivers of the conspiracy theory, the content shared, and the strategies to mitigate the spread of it. Our results are likely to be of international interest during the unfolding COVID-19 pandemic. A further strength of our study is that our methodology can be applied to other conspiracy topics. A limitation of our study is that the Search API can only retrieve data from public facing Twitter accounts. Previous research has noted that certain Twitter topics are likely to contain automated accounts known as "bots"[35]; for instance, in the case of electronic cigarette (e-cigarette) tweets, research has found that social bots could be used to promote new e-cigarette products and spread the idea that they are helpful for smoking cessation.[35] A limitation of our study is that we did not identify social bot accounts; however, influential accounts in our study did not appear to display bot behavior (eg, high number of tweets posted) and appeared to display characteristics of genuine accounts. This could be inferred because certain accounts linked to their profile on other platforms such as YouTube. However, future research could seek to identify the ratio of bots to individual accounts related to conspiracy theories. A further limitation is that our content analysis was conducted on English-language tweets, and further research could seek to examine tweets in other languages. Furthermore, a limitation to our study is that, as we retrieved data using a specific keyword, our data may have excluded tweets from users who tweeted about the conspiracy during this time without using our target keyword or hashtag.

The COVID-19 pandemic has been a serious public health challenge for nations around the world. This study conducted an analysis of a conspiracy theory that threatened to potentially undermine public health efforts. We discussed key users and influential web sources during this time, and discussed potential strategies for combating such dangerous misinformation. The analysis reveals that there was a lack of an authority figure who was actively combating such misinformation, and policymakers should insist in efforts to isolate opinions that are based on fake news if they want to avoid public health damage. Future research could seek to conduct a follow-up analysis of Twitter data as the COVID-19 pandemic evolves.

References

1. Jolly G. Middle East respiratory syndrome coronavirus (MERS-CoV). TIJPH 2016 Dec 31;4(4):351-376. [doi: 10.21522/tijph.2013.04.04.art033]
2. Smith RD. Responding to global infectious disease outbreaks: lessons from SARS on the role of risk perception, communication and management. Soc Sci Med 2006 Dec;63(12):3113-3123 [doi: 10.1016/j.socscimed.2006.08.004] [Medline: 16978751]
3. World Health Organization. Middle East respiratory syndrome coronavirus (MERS-CoV) URL: https://www.who.int/ emergencies/mers-cov/en/ [accessed 2020-04-15]
4. Sohrabi C, Alsafi Z, O'Neill N, Khan M, Kerwan A, Al-Jabir A, et al. World Health Organization declares global emergency: a review of the 2019 novel coronavirus (COVID-19). Int J Surg 2020 Apr;76:71-76 [doi: 10.1016/j.ijsu.2020.02.034] [Medline: 32112977]
5. Wu F, Zhao S, Yu B, Chen Y, Wang W, Song Z, et al. A new coronavirus associated with human respiratory disease in China. Nature 2020 Mar;579(7798):265-269 [doi: 10.1038/s41586-020-2008-3] [Medline: 32015508]
6. Livingston E, Bucher K. Coronavirus disease 2019 (COVID-19) in Italy. JAMA 2020 Mar 17:e. [doi: 10.1001/jama.2020.4344] [Medline: 32181795]
7. Agiwal M, Roy A, Saxena N. Next generation 5G wireless networks: a comprehensive survey. IEEE Commun Surv Tutorials 2016 Feb 19;18(3):1617-1655. [doi: 10.1109/comst.2016.2532458]
8. Quinn B. The Guardian. 2020. Facebook Acts to Halt Far-Right Groups Linking Covid-19 to 5G URL: https://www. theguardian.com/world/2020/apr/12 /facebook-acts-to-halt-far-right-groups-linking-covid-19-to-5g [accessed 2020-04-21]
9. Kelion L. BBC News. 2020 Apr 04. Mast fire probe amid 5G coronavirus claims URL: https://www.bbc.com/news/ uk-england-52164358# [accessed 2020-04-13]
10. Brewis H. Evening Standard. 2020 Apr 14. Nightingale hospital phone mast attacked as 5G conspiracy theory rages on URL: https://www.standard.co.uk/news/uk/nhs -nightingale-phone-mast-arson-attack-5g-conspiracy-a4414351.html
11. Lewis K. Full Fact. 2020 Mar 31. 5G is not accelerating the spread of the new coronavirus URL: https://fullfact.org/health/ 5G-not-accelerating-coronavirus/ [accessed 2020-04-14]
12. Shanapinda S. The Conversation. 2020 Apr 07. No, 5G radiation doesn't cause or spread the coronavirus. Saying it does is destructive URL: https://tinyurl.com /uppng7w [accessed 2020-04-14]
13. Waterson J, Hern A. The Guardian. 2020 Apr 06. At least 20 UK phone masts vandalised over false 5G coronavirus claims URL: https://tinyurl.com/v3fv7mh
14. Chew C, Eysenbach G. Pandemics in the age of Twitter: content analysis of Tweets during the 2009 H1N1 outbreak. PLoS One 2010 Nov 29;5(11):e14118. [doi: 10.1371/journal.pone.0014118] [Medline: 21124761]
15. Li J, Xu Q, Cuomo R, Purushothaman V, Mackey T. Data mining and content analysis of the Chinese social media platform Weibo during the early COVID-19 outbreak: retrospective observational infoveillance study. JMIR Public Health Surveill 2020 Apr 21;6(2):e18700. [doi: 10.2196/18700] [Medline: 32293582]
16. Ahmed W, Lugovic S. Social media analytics: analysis and visualisation of news diffusion using NodeXL. Online Information Review 2019 Feb 11;43(1):149-160. [doi: 10.1108/oir-03-2018-0093]
17. Smith MA, Rainie L, Himelboim I, Shneiderman B. Pew Research Center. 2014 Feb 20. Mapping Twitter topic networks: from polarized crowds to community clusters

URL: https://www.pewresearch.org/internet/2014/02/20/ mapping-twitter-topic -networks-from-polarized-crowds-to-community-clusters/

18. Ahmed W, Marin-Gomez X, Vidal-Alaball J. Contextualising the 2019 e-cigarette health scare: insights from Twitter. Int J Environ Res Public Health 2020 Mar 26;17(7):e, [doi: 10.3390/ijerph17072236] [Medline: 32225020]
19. Ahmed W. Public health implications of #ShoutYourAbortion. Public Health 2018 Oct;163:35-41. [doi: 10.1016/j.puhe.2018.06.010] [Medline: 30059806]
20. Shelley M, Krippendorff K. Content analysis: an introduction to its methodology. J Am Stat Assoc 1984 Mar;79(385):240. [doi: 10.2307/2288384]
21. Ahmed W, Bath P, Demartini G. Using Twitter as a data source: an overview of ethical, legal, and methodological challenge. Adv Res Ethics Integrity 2017:79. [doi: 10.1108/s2398-601820180000002004]
22. White DR, Borgatti SP. Betweenness centrality measures for directed graphs. Soc Networks 1994 Oct;16(4):335-346. [doi: 10.1016/0378-8733(94)90015-9]
23. InfoWars. URL: https://www.infowars.com/
24. RayGuardNJ. URL: https://rayguardnj.com/
25. Stillness in the Storm. URL: https://stillnessinthestorm.com/
26. 5G Crisis. URL: https://www.5gcrisis.com/
27. YouTube. Jeff censored! URL: https://www.youtube.com/channel/ UCAI2PPsCuPRM6KDbwJvSU9A
28. Downing J, Ahmed W. #MacronLeaks as a "warning shot" for European democracies: challenges to election blackouts presented by social media and election meddling during the 2017 French presidential election, Fr Polit 2019 Jun 13,17(3):257-278. [doi: 10.1057/s41253-019-00090-w]
29. Downing J, Dron R. Tweeting Grenfell: discourse and networks in critical constructions of British Muslim social boundaries on social media. New Media Soc 2019 Jul 26;22(3):449-469. [doi: 10.1177/1461444819864572]
30. Allcott H, Gentzkow M. Social media and fake news in the 2016 election. J Econ Perspect 2017 May;31(2):211-236. [doi: 10.1257/jep.31.2.211]
31. Nussbaum E. The New Yorker. 2017 Jan 23. How jokes won the election URL: https:// www.newyorker.com/magazine/2017/01/23/how-jokes-won-the-election
32. Wolfsfeld G, Segev E, Sheafer T. Social Media and the Arab Spring. Int J of Press/Polit 2013 Jan 16;18(2):115-137. [doi: 10.1177/1940161212471716]
33. Sifry ML. WikiLeaks and the Age of Transparency. New York: OR Books; 2011.
34. Tidy J. BBC News. 2020 Apr 16. Coronavirus: Facebook alters virus action after damning misinformation report URL: https://www.bbc.com/news /technology-52309094
35. Allem J, Ferrara E. The importance of debiasing social media data to better understand e-cigarette-related attitudes and behaviors. J Med Internet Res 2016 Aug 09;18(8):e219. [doi: 10.2196/jmir.6185] [Medline: 27507563]

Viewpoint 5

> *"Doctors, psychologists, and social workers should encourage health professionals to attend continuous training activities demystifying conspiracy theories and how to address them when confronted with an individual endorsing them."*

Conspiracy Theories Are a Public Health Concern

Marie-Jeanne Leonard and Frederick L. Philippe

In the following viewpoint, Marie-Jeanne Leonard and Frederick L. Philippe argue that conspiracy theories can lead to radicalization, which has turned out to be an important public health issue. The authors claim that the COVID-19 pandemic created fear and frustration, motivating many individuals to search for a narrative that would explain the pandemic. The conspiracy theories are a reflection of the lack of trust that many people have in the government. Marie-Jeanne Leonard is on the faculty of psychology and education at the University of Porto in Portugal. Frederick L. Philippe is affiliated with the University of Bamberg in Germany.

"Conspiracy Theories: A Public Health Concern and How to Address It," by Marie-Jeanne Leonard and Frederick L. Philippe, *Frontiers in Psychology*, July 28, 2021, https://doi.org/10.3389/fpsyg.2021.682931.

As you read, consider the following questions:

1. What is narrative as defined in the viewpoint, and what is its relevance to conspiracy theories?
2. What three public health concerns does conspiracy endorsement feed, according to the authors?
3. What importance does accountability have in combatting conspiracy theories?

The SARS-CoV-2 pandemic was characterized by a significant increase in the endorsement of conspiracy theories. Conspiracy theories are narratives that can enable and accentuate distrust toward health professionals and authorities. As such, they can lead to violent radicalization and should be considered a public health issue. This perspective article aims to further the understanding of professionals on conspiracy theories via the 3N model of radicalization and self-determination theory. Based on empirical research, theory, and existing interventions, potential initiatives intended to tackle the issue of conspiracy theories during pandemics are also presented.

Introduction

Increasingly, people around the globe grow tired and frustrated in response to lockdowns and health measures that are meant to counter the ongoing SARS-CoV-2 pandemic. This angst is partly manifested through the increased popularity of conspiracy theories (European Commission, 2020). An international survey carried out in 28 countries revealed that one-third of people worldwide believe that "a foreign power/other force" consciously caused the current pandemic (e.g., 18, 58, and 26% believe so in the United Kingdom, Bulgaria, and Thailand, respectively; Gallup International Association, 2020). Such conspiracy beliefs represent public health issues contributing to the fracture of the trust civilians hold toward government officials and health professionals, a phenomenon that has been observed during other disease outbreaks (Cohn and Kutalek, 2016). The objective of this perspective article is to improve the understanding of conspiracy theories, to discuss how they impact the population, and to highlight potential ways to intervene during pandemics based on theory, empirical research, and existing interventions.

We argue that conspiracy theories should be considered as narratives that can lead to violent radicalization and, as such, this phenomenon represents an important public health issue. Conspiracy theories are better understood via the 3N model of radicalization (Kruglanski et al., 2019) and self-determination theory (Ryan and Deci, 2017). The 3N model specifies three pillars in the radicalization process that align with the understanding of conspiracy theories (i.e., need, narrative, and network), while self-determination theory deepens the understanding of the need pillar.

Conspiracy Theories

Need refers to the motivation to recover significance following its loss due to an adverse event (Kruglanski et al., 2019). Specifically, this significance loss can be conceptualized as the thwarting of three psychological needs that were found to be universal: competence, autonomy, and relatedness (Ryan and Deci, 2017). Indeed, the satisfaction or frustration of these three psychological needs influences how people perceive and react to an event (Ryan and Deci, 2017). The satisfaction of these psychological needs is considered as a continual quest, and when they are not satisfied or are frustrated, people naturally seek to fulfill them (Sheldon and Gunz, 2009; Ryan and Deci, 2017). They are, therefore, considered as core determinants of motivation that lead one to act on their environment and to carry certain objectives (Sheldon and Gunz, 2009; Ryan and Deci, 2017). Conspiracy theories unfold following an important event that hinders the perception of control of an individual (autonomy), the ability of an individual to make sense of the world (competence), and connectedness of an individual (relatedness; Ryan and Deci, 2017; van Prooijen, 2020). In 2020, many countries enforced a lockdown for months, a significant event that precipitated economic uncertainty and restrained individual freedom. Many have perceived their basic needs as thwarted as they lost control over their usual occupations, they were cut off from their loved ones, and authorities disseminated mixed messages because they did not (and still do not) fully understand the new virus. Such stressful events are likely to reactivate the recall of past personal life events that were need thwarting in a similar fashion (e.g., experiences of ostracism, natural disasters, or other traumas), thus exacerbating the current thus exacerbating the thwarted needs related to the pandemic experience (Philippe and Houle, 2020). A vulnerability to the reactivation of such need thwarting memories can motivate one to retrieve significance by finding compensatory ways to fulfill those needs, making one cognitively receptive to new narratives.

Conspiracy theories are a form of Narrative, defined as a shared belief system providing an alternative ideological framework to explain a situation and offer guidance as to how to behave to regain significance, control, and affiliations (Kruglanski et al., 2019). As conspiracy theories are alternative narratives to the status quo, people turn to them to compensate for their thwarted needs. Such narratives accentuate the threatening characteristics of demonized outgroups and praise the people who endorse the beliefs and behaviors put forward by the ideology, hence cognitively and behaviorally polarizing believers (Kruglanski et al., 2019). Of note, some authors have suggested that believing in conspiracy theories can be adaptive to survival (van Prooijen, 2020); however, one could argue that such beliefs could be considered adaptive only when they concern real conspiracies and not unjustified conspiracy theories. In the past, some conspiracies were proved to be real, rendering it difficult to distinguish unjustified conspiracy theories from real conspiracies. Unjustified conspiracy theories are not adaptive for survival, as they can be detrimental to the health of others and the individual (e.g., SARS-CoV-2 being a hoax, vaccines being dangerous, etc.). The European Commission (2020) characterizes real conspiracies as focusing on a specific event or individual, such as an assassination, and based on valid proof and facts brought forward by "whistle-blowers and the media." The European Commission (2020) adds that whistle-blowers recognize the extent and limitations of their knowledge instead of being rigid and absolute about it. On the other hand, unjustified conspiracy theories are characterized by five distinctive elements: pattern, agency, coalition, threat, and secrecy (van Prooijen and van Vugt, 2018). Such narratives are not parsimonious and detail a pattern establishing causal relationships between multiple events, people, and/or objects (van Prooijen and van Vugt, 2018). These narratives also imply agency, that is, they attribute intentions to malevolent and malicious groups of people who form a coalition and who have a deliberate plan that represents a threat to the ingroup (van Prooijen and van Vugt, 2018). Above all else, these theories are characterized by a secrecy element, which makes them irrefutable.

When one adheres to a narrative, they then seek the presence of like-minded individuals, forming a network (Kruglanski et al., 2019). In the past few months, those who endorsed a conspiracy theory on SARS-CoV-2 connected via social media, creating echo chambers. These echo chambers spread the reinforcement of both individual and collective actions that exacerbated tensions between civilians and impeded the initiatives of authorities to halt the propagation of the virus around the globe, propelling actions such as civil disobedience, maskless demonstrations, or a refusal to get tested and vaccinated.

Conspiracy theories and their associated actions are endorsed to satisfy the thwarted needs and fulfill the lost sense of significance. However, conspiracy theories are not expected to truly satisfy the basic needs, they potentially, only temporarily, compensate for them. Research has indeed found that when needs are experienced as frustrated, they lead the individual to rigidly engage in activities that appear to overcome some of the insecurities and threats stemming from need frustration, but this engagement falls short of achieving this and often leads to worst consequences (for a review, refer to Vansteenkiste et al., 2020). Empirical data suggest that conspiracy theories may cultivate the thwarting of the basic needs, creating a feedback loop in which the person is further reinforced to support and expand their beliefs in conspiracy theories (Douglas et al., 2017; van Prooijen, 2020). For instance, it has been shown that exposure to conspiracy theories decreases the feelings of control and autonomy by increasing perceptions of powerlessness (Jolley and Douglas, 2014a,b; Douglas et al., 2017). This is not surprising given that, although conspiracy theories offer an alternative explanation to adverse events, they emphasize how the actions of individuals cannot have an impact on the status quo, possibly further thwarting the need for autonomy. They also highlight how numerous events, people, and objects are interrelated, as well as how the truth is hidden from the public, likely frustrating the sense of competence of individuals. Eventually, conspiracy theories can increase the feeling of being socially alienated, as they underscore how the ingroup is badly treated by the outgroup and how the ingroup is the target of threatening plans. In addition, conspiracy theories are often a source of interpersonal conflicts between conspiracy believers and non-believers, possibly negatively affecting relationships and friendships and further reinforcing the frustration of the need for relatedness.

Past Health Crises and Conspiracy Theories

Past health crises provide some insights into the development of conspiracy theories concerning viruses. The element of mistrust toward mainstream media, influential figures, authorities, and/or governmental institutions was the most recurring theme reported to facilitate the endorsement and spread of conspiracy theories throughout past epidemics as various as the Zika (Kou et al., 2017; Smallman, 2018), Ebola (Masumbuko Claude et al., 2019; Vinck et al., 2019), or H1N1 (Smallman, 2015). Many of these virus-related conspiracies revolved around capitalistic ill-intentions among powerful individuals (Smallman, 2015, 2018; Masumbuko Claude et al., 2019).

Trust can be modulated by real conspiracies unveiled in the past, past persecutions, and disparities perpetrated by authority figures toward minority groups (Smallman, 2015, 2018; Abramowitz et al., 2017; Kou et al., 2017) or by how authorities and institutions are perceived to competently manage an epidemic (Masumbuko Claude et al., 2019). In addition, we argue that mistrust toward institutions and the government could be a pre-epidemic social symptom engendered by past experiences of need frustration (e.g., social ostracism and injustice), which could be triggered or exacerbated by a health crisis and subjectively experienced as mistrust due to the loss of significance. This mistrust could then be further affected by how authorities and policymakers alienate the psychological needs of the population through their management of a health crisis and the enforcement of sociosanitary measures. This lack of trust is to be taken seriously, as it has been associated with a higher risk of not complying with measures and behaviors intended to contain the spread of a virus (e.g., refusing to get vaccinated, avoiding to consult with a health professional, etc. Vinck et al., 2019).

A Public Health Concern

There is a dire need for official authorities worldwide to tackle this issue, as conspiracy endorsement feeds at least three clear public health concerns. First, the actions perpetrated by conspiracy believers increase the risk of contracting and propagating SARS-CoV-2 among the population, which, unsurprisingly, puts resources and financial pressures on health care systems. In addition, conspiracy theories can have economic repercussions at an individual level. Individuals of low socioeconomic status can see their financial struggles increase due to influential conspiracy leaders who tend to ask for financial donations to fund their organizations and to continue promoting their alternative narratives. Financial donations are often portrayed by conspiracy narratives as a way to restore the lost sense of significance. Last, people integrating conspiracy theories as core beliefs should be of high concern for governmental representatives and health professionals. Such core beliefs increase the likelihood of one endorsing other conspiracy theories and networks in the long run (van Prooijen, 2020), potentially further bolstering their distrust and rejection of traditional medicine (e.g., vaccines, treatments, and basic hygienic measures).

Potential Initiatives

Policymakers and authorities should be careful to not circulate mixed and confusing messages at a given time (Abramowitz et al., 2017), as past epidemics were marked by the dissemination of ambivalent messages on the virus at play (Kou et al., 2017). However, changing information is not necessarily synonymous with mixed messages (Carlsen and Glenton, 2016). To prevent their information and messages from being considered as mixed, policymakers and authorities should "acknowledge" the presence of uncertainty and that the information disseminated will be adjusted as time goes by (Carlsen and Glenton, 2016). Otherwise, people might consider and interpret mainstream information as misinformation (Ball and Maxmen, 2020). Furthermore, Ball and Maxmen (2020) emphasized that authorities and policymakers should describe the reasons and rationale that "guide" the changed decisions during an epidemic.

We recommend the following societal and individual-level initiatives to defuse conspiracy beliefs and prevent them from cognitively crystalizing in the long run. These initiatives are conceived from empirical studies, professional reports, and successful measures involved in the adequate handling of past epidemics (Niang, 2015; Cohn and Kutalek, 2016; Baggio et al., 2019; Sigfrid et al., 2020). Studies have suggested that increasing the sense of control, perception of transparency, and self-affirmation (i.e., asserting the values, meaning, and feelings of an individual) can decrease the strength of conspiracy beliefs (Whitson and Galinski, 2008; Carlsen and Glenton, 2016; Douglas et al., 2017; Poon et al., 2020; van Prooijen, 2020). There is a consensus among professionals that engaging the population and genuinely listening to their needs, perceptions, and concerns greatly helps to ensure the efficacy of sanitary measures during disease outbreaks (Niang, 2015; Cohn and

Kutalek, 2016; Baggio et al., 2019). Indeed, public health measures to contain past Ebola epidemics were varied and included community engagement initiatives (Coltart et al., 2017). Though Coltart et al. (2017) consider it unclear which initiatives worked best, as they were usually implemented at the same time, the authors highlighted that community engagement initiatives seem to act as a catalyst to other initiatives (Coltart et al., 2017). Community engagement measures potentially work by increasing trust toward authorities, therefore increasing compliance and adequate function of other public health measures (Coltart et al., 2017).

Therefore, we first strongly advise state and local governments to invest in the implementation of a "qualitative community feedback mechanism" as was implemented for instance by the Democratic Republic of Congo as an additional measure for Ebola epidemics (Baggio et al., 2019; Nachega et al., 2020). This mechanism collected perceptions and comments of people about the epidemic (i.e., Ebola) to (1) improve trust and engagement of communities and (2) help officials with feedback to adapt their decisions and priorities in terms of the needs of the community (Baggio et al., 2019). The information collected by the feedback mechanism was afterward coded, analyzed, and shared with the adequate authorities (Baggio et al., 2019). Such a mechanism allows each citizen to feel part of the larger social network and favors community engagement and empowerment, elements identified as key targets during an epidemic to reduce fears and rumors (Cohn and Kutalek, 2016; Baggio et al., 2019; Sigfrid et al., 2020). Therefore, state and local governments should ensure their population the universal access to a feedback mechanism regarding SARS-CoV-2 so that all can demonstrate self-affirmation by expressing their thoughts, perceptions, and questions about the current pandemic (Poon et al., 2020; van Prooijen, 2020). Special advisors should be appointed to oversee the mechanism and the adequate communication between involved parties (Sigfrid et al., 2020). State and local governments should also take the time to publicly and transparently respond to questions and comments raised via the feedback mechanism (including recognizing the limitations of government in understanding SARS-CoV-2), thus demonstrating that concerns of civilians are considered in the decision-making process (Niang, 2015; Baggio et al., 2019). The aim should not simply be to convince people of the "truth" but rather to create a bidirectional communication system allowing a true connection of trust between civilians and officials (O'Malley et al., 2009) and acknowledge the emotional stress induced by the current situation. This type of mechanism would support the needs for autonomy, competence, and relatedness and would therefore potentially reconnect one with truthful information regarding SARS-CoV-2 (Goldberg and Richley, 2020).

Second, at a micro-level, when health professionals face a person who endorses a conspiracy theory, we strongly recommend them to open a non-judgmental dialogue and instill a sense of trust in the relationship. Given the premise that endorsed conspiracy beliefs are a failed attempt to satisfy thwarted needs, these dialogues represent an opportunity that must be grasped (1) to let the person express their beliefs in a safe environment, (2) to respectfully offer rational counter-arguments if necessary, (3) to rationally explore why the counter-arguments are frustrating and how the conspiracy beliefs could keep one frustrated in terms of autonomy, competence, and/or relatedness, and (4) to investigate healthy ways to fulfill the needs so that the person can reconnect with others (Niang, 2015; Orosz et al., 2016). Such actions have the potential to satisfy the initially thwarted needs, therefore curbing the influence of conspiracy beliefs.

Finally, not all believers in conspiracy theories are on the track to radicalization. Kou et al. (2017) described how "in the face of crisis, people face enormous uncertainty and have urgent information needs," which translates into important needs for autonomy and competence. Some, in a quest for "collective sensemaking," (Kou et al., 2017) were only deceived by fake news advertised on social media or were misinformed by a trusted close other (European Commission, 2020). Around the world, some countries tried to counter distrust regarding SARS-CoV-2 by employing fear campaigns that advertised threatening health messages, further frustrating the need for competence and autonomy (Stolow et al., 2020). Research suggests that these campaigns are ineffective, as they are experienced as controlling and only extrinsically motivate one to comply with the recommended health measures (Williams et al., 1999). They often have a short-term modest effect (Tannenbaum et al., 2015), mostly among people who are already in agreement with the message, but they fail to change the behaviors of the target group for which they were developed (Ruiter et al., 2014). Instead, authorities should employ rumor detectors (Baggio et al., 2019) specifically targeting fake news regarding the pandemic. Such a detector would have the potential to provide tailored information based on the misunderstandings of the population and unfounded rumors not reported via the qualitative community feedback mechanism. Based on this detector, authorities could make a weekly review and disseminate it to the media (e.g., editorials and radio stations) to inform the general population and disseminate it to elementary, high school, and college professors to ensure the circulation of adequate and truthful information among youth.

Getting Policymakers to Implement Changes

At the moment, there is a need to raise awareness of policymakers on the issue of conspiracy endorsement. To do so, we strongly encourage researchers and other professionals working in the field of conspiracy to increase their presence in the media (e.g., via radio hosts and journalists) to circulate reliable information and to get the conversation going on the issue of conspiracy endorsement (Burstein, 2003). By raising the salience of the issue and by changing the public opinion on this issue, the chances of getting the attention of policymakers increase (Burstein, 2003). In addition, more articles and materials written in lay language are needed (Economic and Social Research Council, 2021). Such articles and material could be tailored for publishing in daily newspapers known to be read by policymakers (e.g., *The Hill Times* in Ottawa, Canada). The members of the public who feel concerned by the issue of conspiracy endorsement should be encouraged to lobby and/or to solicitate their local or state government representatives via emails, phone calls, and in-person meetings to encourage the implementation of preventive initiatives. The civic engagement action of lobbying could even increase the satisfaction of the three psychological needs by rallying members of the public with an objective, providing a sense of self-efficacy, and producing a sense of control within their society.

To increase awareness and highlight the scale of the issue of conspiracy endorsement in the population, we further propose that researchers investigate the societal costs generated by conspiracy endorsement and their associated behaviors. Such societal costs would include the direct costs related to mental health issues and the actions associated with endorsed conspiracy theories, including health services used due to mental and/or physical health issues and their indirect impact on loss of productivity at work and job turnover. The direct costs could be two-fold; on the one hand, people who endorse conspiracy theories are at risk of refusing and avoiding traditional health care services (including refusing vaccines) in favor of alternative medicines, which could have long-term impacts on their health and the spread of viruses in the general population. On the other hand, the development of long-term diseases and/or the development of mental health issues could have a direct economic impact on health care services used (e.g., emergency room visits, hospitalizations, psychiatric hospitalization, and medication use).

The understanding of health professionals on conspiracy theories should also be actualized and updated. Professional orders (i.e., doctors, psychologists, and socials workers) should encourage health professionals to attend continuous training activities demystifying conspiracy theories and how to address them when confronted with an individual endorsing them.

Accountability and Transparency

Given the importance of the issue of mistrust toward authorities, the handling of actions perpetrated by governments and health professionals that can reinforce conspiracy theories is to be considered. Indeed, past conspiracies that were revealed as true have served as fuel for the current unjustified conspiracy theories circulating (e.g., Tuskegee experiment, Wikileaks, etc.; Smallman, 2018; Pierre, 2020). To facilitate the implementation of the proposed initiatives and increase trust, authorities and policymakers should support and value the concepts of accountability and transparency (Coltart et al., 2017). Accountability is important to value due to the secrecy element characterizing conspiracy theories. Government officials, medical professionals, researchers, and any other authority figures who perpetrated and/or caused the persecution of a group, intentionally or not, should be publicly held accountable. Covering up past and present faults only risks amplifying the secrecy element of conspiracy theories and reinforcing their endorsement and generalization. The other key element, transparency, has been pointed by multiple authors as a critical principle with which to manage public health concerns, including epidemics, which are events of tremendous uncertainty (O'Malley et al., 2009; Carlsen and Glenton, 2016). Governments holding back information increase the risk that people "collectively generate alternative narratives" (Kou et al., 2017). Carlsen and Glenton (2016) reported similar conclusions and highlighted the importance of being transparent regarding the rationale of strategies used and the reasons for the decisions taken. Based on their systematic review of qualitative studies, Carlsen and Glenton (2016) believe that "transparency regarding uncertainty" would lead to "compliance with public health strategies."

Discussion

The present article asserted that conspiracy theories are narratives that can lead to violent radicalization via the thwarting of the universal needs of autonomy, competence, and relatedness. There is a consensus among experts that mistrust toward government representatives and authorities is central to the spreading of conspiracy theories during epidemics. Such mistrust toward authorities and influential figures could reflect the repetitive thwarting of needs. Accordingly, initiatives promoting community engagement are considered essential to ensure compliance with health measures during epidemics and to reduce the prevalence of endorsement of conspiracy theories; however, the best approach to regain trust is unknown (Vinck et al., 2019). The initiatives presented in this article aim to increase community engagement and trust toward authorities by satisfying the needs for autonomy, competence, and relatedness; however, they do require a certain basic level of trust from the population, which is a limitation to their potential efficacy. It is therefore not possible at the moment to determine the level of efficacy of the presented initiatives. To try to ensure their efficacy, governments will have to multiply their voices at various places simultaneously and deliver consistent messages and information. Governments could also collaborate with alternative and local leadership figures present in the population (e.g., athletes, influencers, and religious figures, Coltart et al., 2017; Vinck et al., 2019). We encourage that the implementation of the proposed initiatives is paired up with an assessment of their usefulness and efficacy.

Some governments have already implemented channels of communication through which people can raise their concerns and ask questions (e.g., public consultations with the population and government representative talks including question periods). However, the effectiveness of these channels of communication can be hindered, as some governments do not end up holding their end of the bargain and implement the changes promised. If governments do not listen to the concerns of their population, transparently communicate, and support the satisfaction of the needs of the population for autonomy, competence, and relatedness, one unavoidable consequence is that the endorsement of conspiracy theories will increase and, therefore, negatively affect the public health of their population.

What Are Other Well-Known Conspiracy Theories?

Chapter Preface

QAnon is not the only conspiracy theory floating around online. There are hundreds if not thousands of others, prevalent in any and every aspect of society, from government to mysterious disappearances to aliens to aviation to even sports.

The viewpoints in the following chapter explore some of the best-known conspiracy theories, such as the flat-Earth conspiracy, the Illuminati, and the Bermuda Triangle. They also cover the intrinsic connections between conspiracy theories and religion, especially the anti-Semitic rhetoric lurking in many unfounded theories.

This chapter also explores one of the earliest, well-known precursors to the QAnon conspiracy theory: the 2011 Barack Obama birtherism conspiracy theory perpetuated by Donald Trump in the years before his decision to run for president. Featured in Obama's memoir, *A Promised Land*, the story of Trump's insistence that Obama was not a natural-born US citizen was the country's first taste in how unfounded claims can be perpetuated and be even legitimized by the media.

Additionally, this chapter explores the connections between Christians and conspiracy theories, including why some sects of Christianity are more susceptible to believing in these vast conspiracies.

One of the keys to a lasting conspiracy theory is that it must be broad, which makes it both challenging to prove and to disprove, and the belief tends to be unwavering and a challenge to break.

> *"A disturbing number of professing Christians are entranced by macabre QAnon conspiracies, anti-vaccination hysteria, unverifiable claims of stolen elections or bizarre fantasies regarding the nefarious machinations of Bill Gates."*

Christians Seem More Willing to Embrace Conspiracy Theories

Steven Willing

In the following viewpoint, Steven Willing explores why Christians specifically tend to believe in conspiracy theories. The viewpoint explores the four factors behind these beliefs. It also explores some of the most common conspiracy theories outside of the QAnon conspiracy theory that gripped the United States during the 2020 election cycle. The author features stories of conspiracy theories like the foundation of the antivaccination movement—a debunked study by former Dr. Andrew Wakefield published in 1999 that fraudulently connected the MMR vaccine to autism. Additionally, the viewpoint details how conspiracy theories are not just found on social media, but also inside the spiritual realm, where religion is founded and focused. Dr. Steven Willing is a medical doctor who also holds an MBA and is an adjunct professor of divinity at Regent University.

"Christians and Conspiracy Theories," by Steven Willing, Christian Medical & Dental Associations, February 18, 2021. Reprinted by permission.

As you read, consider the following questions:

1. According to the viewpoint, why do Christians so often believe in conspiracy theories and especially find the QAnon conspiracy theory so believable?
2. What are the four factors behind belief in conspiracy theories and how they resonate with people no matter what religion, according to the author?
3. Why do bad actors intentionally choose to create and spread conspiracies?

"You can't handle the truth!"

That classic line from *A Few Good Men* from Colonel Jessup in the witness stand became a waving flag for many. It is enticing to think we own the truth, and that those who can't "handle" it are naïve, weak or cowardly. Delivered to perfection by Jack Nicholson, Jessup hammered a wedge between truth and fantasy, and of course we all know which side we're on, don't we?

What most overlook is that Colonel Jessup was fooling himself. Yes, the character was a courageous leader with a distinguished career, but he was also a vindictive bully who fought to suppress the truth about his own culpability in the death of Private Santiago.

The fall of humanity commenced with an assault on truth, and it sometimes feels the battle against truth has never been more relentless. Among followers of Christ, this should be obvious. We witness in the secular culture a frequent denial of reality: whether it's the humanity of the unborn, the immutability of sex or the facts of history. Our reaction might range from despair to compassion to mockery, but too often we forget these are lost souls under the dominion of dark spiritual forces. So, what's our excuse?

Why do so many of our brothers and sisters in the Lord commit the same denial of reality they mock in unbelievers?

Christians and Conspiracy Theories

A disturbing number of professing Christians are entranced by macabre QAnon conspiracies, anti-vaccination hysteria, unverifiable claims of stolen elections (from both sides of the partisan divide) or bizarre fantasies regarding the nefarious machinations of Bill Gates.

Much digital "ink" has been spilt over the last 12 months on Christians and conspiracies, though it is difficult to tell whether this has had much impact. Those most inclined toward conspiracy theories are the least likely to read or to benefit from the articles. Most articles have focused on refuting the specific conspiracies or warning of the moral implications. Still others will tell you how to avoid them. Such articles may help protect fence-sitters from plunging into the abyss. The problem is that too many proponents don't care. Explaining to a conspiracy hound how to tell truth from fiction is like teaching my dog how to eat healthy: he doesn't see the point, he's sure it doesn't apply to him and the conversation's going nowhere.

To better understand the issue, we must look beyond what they believe to why they believe. Popular myths comprise a broad category, of which conspiracy theories are merely a subset. The principles we will examine apply across the spectrum.

The Gospels report that after the resurrection of Christ, the priests conspired with the Roman guards to report that the disciples stole the body (Matthew 28:11-15). So, conspiracy theories have been around as long as conspiracies, and in this case, we have a twofer—a real conspiracy by the priests and guards to spread a false conspiracy theory concerning the disciples. But this historical example exhibits elements true for the 21st century as well as the first. Conspiracy theories don't pop out of nowhere. Often, they are instigated by bad actors with ulterior motives who know they are untrue.

Why They Resonate with Us

This problem is far more nuanced than simply dismissing conspiracy theorists as gullible and uncritical thinkers. Indeed, many are, but forces in our own mental programming and our environment strongly drive us in that direction.

Humans are curious by nature. God designed us to seek understanding and explanations. With diligent effort, a broad fund of knowledge and the wisdom of experience, this often works. The blessing of a curious nature led to the spectacular technological progress of the last few centuries. We don't just want to know how nature works. We want to understand how people work, why things happen and why people do the things they do. Serious sociology and psychology—there's a lot of unserious work in both fields—are responsible and efficient means to satisfy this impulse. So are forensics and fields of legal investigation. Conspiracy theories, on the other hand, are a cheat, a short cut into a blind alley. One hundred hours of watching YouTube videos are no substitute for years of education, but they are quite efficient in fostering unjustified confidence. They might be wildly off base, but for meeting the explanatory impulse they are equally effective and sometimes more emotionally fulfilling than the boring truth (for reasons considered below).

A second force is almost certainly the biasing effect of entertainment. Over our lifetimes, we consume thousands of hours of film and television drama, and, more often than not, some dark conspiracy is underfoot. If we pause to reflect (thinking with Kahnemen's System 2), we might admit that these are rare in real life, but we do most of our thinking in System 1, which is heuristically driven and powerfully influenced by non-rational factors such as recency and ease of recall. So, if day after day, week after week, year after year we are fed conspiracy stories, they are bound to seem more plausible. How do you think Hollywood changed public attitudes toward homosexuality in such a short period of time?

The third factor is the unprecedented availability of misinformation and disinformation enabled by the internet. Old barriers to publication and distribution have been eliminated and everyone now has a platform. Engineers at Twitter, Facebook and Instagram developed systems that focus and amplify the impact of misinformation, though that was not their intent. We naturally want our opinions confirmed, and complicated algorithms are specifically designed to keep you engaged by telling you more and more of what you want to hear, while you are guaranteed to be surrounded and supported by like-minded company.

A fourth issue that must be acknowledged is that conspiracies really do happen. True conspiracies are rare. Many authors have explained why they are rare, seldom succeed and how to spot the fake ones. Nonetheless, the simple fact that some have happened affords the true believer "moral license" to believe in one or more that are purely fictitious.

Sinful Disposition

Unfortunately, not all internal factors inclining us toward conspiracy theories are so innocent and defensible. There is a dark element to many that appeals directly to the vilest of human impulses.

Conspiracy theories feed our ego. The sense of superiority that comes from being "in the know" can be intoxicating. Like Neo in *The Matrix*, proponents imagine themselves escaping the blinders of society by taking "the red pill" and becoming the hero of their own pathetic little fiction. The act of embracing a lie to become something greater was the offense of Adam, and in this we are truly his offspring.

Some anti-vaccination activists focus on past use of one or two fetal cell lines in vaccine development. (The morality of this has been fully addressed by a number of authorities, including CMDA). There's no clear boundary between having a sensitive conscience and overt moral grandstanding, and the feeling I get having observed and interacted with many of these activists is that they know they are morally superior to other Christians and they want everyone else to know it as well.

Conspiracy theories malign our enemies and justify our prejudice. Among all conspiracy theories, the bloodiest, most contemptible and most enduring must be those surrounding the children of Abraham. From being blamed for the bubonic plague in the 14th century, to accusations of conspiring with the enemy in late 19th century France, to the wildest fantasies of an uber-rich and uber-powerful global cabal, the Jews have suffered the most from conspiracy thinking, and they experienced the deadly power of lies with six million deaths under the Third Reich.

Anti-semitism appeals to some of the worst human impulses—to feel superior to those who are different, to justify our prejudices, to rationalize our own conduct and to absolve us of personal responsibility for failure. Adolf Hitler rose to power by blaming the Jews for every real and perceived shortcoming of early 20th century Germany, including their loss in World War I. A newly elected congresswomen from Georgia blamed the 2018 California wildfires on Jewish space lasers, rhetoric described as "inflammatory" by the *Wall Street Journal* in an apparently unintentional act of punnery.

Anti-vaccination activists presume almost all of the millions of worldwide physicians who both prescribe and use them are either stupid or malevolent. Righteous people do not believe such things.

Willful Deception

For many, many reasons we are predisposed toward embracing conspiracy theories. We are the demand side of the marketplace. On the supply side is a vast industry of private and state actors competing for profit, fame or influence, and they are eager to provide.

There are bad actors out there with an intent to deceive and the means to do so. The anti-vaccination movement traces its roots to the work of the former Dr. Andrew Wakefield, who published a paper in *Lancet* in 1999 claiming to have found a connection between the MMR vaccine and autism. Later investigation established that the research was fraudulent, that Wakefield had to have known and that he was motivated financially by the promise of riches from the plaintiff's bar. Provocateur and shyster Alex Jones rose to notoriety after September 11 peddling the crackpot notion that the terrorist attack was an inside job executed by the highest levels of government. He is now being sued—one hopes successfully—by the parents of schoolchildren murdered at Sandy Hook, after Jones carried on for months arguing the tragedy was a hoax and the bereaved parents were merely actors. Whether Jones believes such nonsense I neither know nor care, but peddling it to a gullible and willing audience has made him both rich and famous.

Emerging evidence over the last several years has pointed to the involvement of hostile foreign states in manipulating American public opinion. The communist regime of China now exercises near-veto power over American film production, where profits speak louder than principles. (US social media channels are blocked in China, and the local versions are tightly controlled. They're not stupid.) Russian activity on social media in the US and other Western democracies is well documented. Far from the simplistic narrative that they attempted to promote the election of Donald Trump, Russian-promoted social media plays to all extremes of the political spectrum. Their presumed intent has been to promote civil strife, discord, resentment and polarization. They must be thrilled with their apparent success.

Christians who believe Scripture must take seriously another source of deception: the spiritual realm. The spiritual entities at war against God are consistently characterized as both attractive and deceiving. If we believe Scripture, then the battle for truth is much more than an argument with our opponent. It's spiritual warfare that must be fought with spiritual weapons. Jesus didn't cast out demons with superior arguments or by instructing their victims in critical thinking.

"Put on the whole armor of God, that you may be able to stand against the wiles of the devil. For we do not wrestle against flesh and blood, but against principalities, against powers, against the rulers of the darkness of this age, against spiritual hosts of wickedness in the heavenly places" (Ephesians 6:11-12, NKJV).

It requires much less effort to assert a claim than refute it. Conspiracy fans and anti vaxxers never really engage in serious research, though they routinely claim to have done so. "Research," in this instance, amounts to watching hours of video and consuming large doses of polemics manufactured for and posted to fringe websites. Those never make one an expert, but they can make someone feel like one. A little knowledge can seem like a lot when you have no idea how much you don't know. It takes no real effort to blindly accept a list of 20 or 30 assertions and repost them on Facebook, as I've seen so much of in the last year. It takes an extraordinary amount of effort to track down the source of each claim and spot the error. Organizations such as CMDA frequently post careful rebuttals on vaccination myths and health misinformation, but it's a whack-a-mole game with newer and more ridiculous claims surfacing with depressing regularity.

Consequences

Succumbing to such deceptions exacts a great cost for both individuals and the church at large. They corrupt our character, demolish our credibility, lead us to sin against others and place us in alignment with malevolent spiritual forces.

Corrupted character. Conspiratorial thinking thrives on pride, and it nourishes it in turn. It takes a considerable amount of arrogance to assert superior insight over legitimate experts in a field. I have, in turn, been accused of arrogance in dismissing their arguments. Pride exists within all of us to one degree or another, so I stand guilty as charged. However, in this instance, humility is submitting to the judgment of an overwhelming consensus of experts, not standing in opposition to them. Genuine love and yearning for the truth, on the other hand, is a fruit of the Spirit (Ephesians 5:9).

Lost credibility. When either individuals or large sections of the body of Christ become known for embracing and promoting disinformation, we compromise our credibility on the more important issues. The secular community will reason that if we're crazy on one score, the rest must be part of the package. We have a duty to them, and a responsibility to God, to preserve our reputation (1 Peter 2:12).

Slander. Hurling false accusations against other groups or accusations is slander, and an explicit violation of the ninth commandment. Christians should never be known for such conduct, nor for tolerating it in their midst.

We become pawns to the Father of Lies. Scripture is abundantly clear that there is more to reality than what we perceive with our senses, and that a spiritual war has been raging since creation. There is no DMZ in this conflict.

"You are of your father the devil, and the desires of your father you want to do. He was a murderer from the beginning, and does not stand in the truth, because there is no truth in him. When he speaks a lie, he speaks from his own resources, for he is a liar and the father of it" (John 8:44, NKJV).

If we are not on the side of truth, then we are on the side of the enemy. This belief, though, can become deadly when we begin to think we own the truth. The only path along this narrow ledge is to admit our personal limitations and exhibit humble submission toward those in authority—in this case, meaning those most qualified in the subject. We shouldn't rely on pastors in matters of science, we shouldn't rely on scientists in matters of theology and we should seek health advice from our doctor, not the internet.

For those passionate about the truth, the ongoing struggle against misinformation, disinformation and conspiracy thinking can be daunting. The first concluding principle should be to check yourself (Matthew 7:5). The second is that, yes, we are our brother's keeper. How the church should deal with conspiracy theorists is a sensitive and complex matter, but it cannot remain faithful to Christ and passive in this regard. We must understand why people are drawn to them, so that the root causes might be addressed.

Ultimately this is a spiritual battle, but thankfully we are not unarmed against such a challenge (Ephesians 6:10-18).

We think of truth mostly in terms of what we believe. But how we "handle the truth" may be just as much defined by what we choose not to believe, in spite of pressure sometimes coming from nearly every direction. Can we handle the truth? God expects nothing less.

> *"Such [anti-Semitic] beliefs have real consequences."*

Anti-Semitism Lurks Behind Many Modern Conspiracy Theories

Richard J. Evans

In the following viewpoint, Richard J. Evans details the history of many modern conspiracy theories and their connections to the Jewish people. As a minority religious community in Christian Europe, the Jews were blamed for a wide range of events, from the Black Death to the French Revolution. The author goes on to detail how the most notorious anti-Semitic rhetoric originated with the Protocols of the Elders of Zion, allegedly written in 1897 and popularized by its legitimization by Tsar Nicholas II in Russia. Richard J. Evans is regius professor emeritus of history at the University of Cambridge.

As you read, consider the following questions:

1. How did early conspiracy theories spread prior to the invention of the internet?
2. Why are Jews historically common targets for conspiracy theories?
3. How did George Soros become the center of many modern conspiracy theories connected to the Jewish people?

Conspiracy theories are more popular and more widespread in the 21st century than they have ever been. They are powered by the rise of the internet and social media, enabled by the declining influence of traditional gatekeepers of opinion such as newspaper editors, TV executives and book publishers, and encouraged by the spread of the uncertainty about truth and falsehood encapsulated in the perverse concept of "alternative facts" popularised by, among others, former US president Donald Trump and his spokespeople.

Over the centuries conspiracy theories have pointed the finger at many different groups, from the Jesuits to the Freemasons, but it is above all Jews who have been the object of the paranoia they represent.

A minority religious community in an overwhelmingly Christian Europe, the Jews were blamed in the Middle Ages and after for a whole range of seemingly inexplicable events, most notably perhaps the Black Death, the pandemic of bubonic plague that killed half Europe's population in 1348-1349, and the French Revolution, which overthrew the traditional European order in the years after 1789. Massacres and pogroms were the result.

It was in Russia under Tsar Nicholas II that the most notorious of anti-Semitic tracts originated. Known as the Protocols of the Elders of Zion, it purported to be the minutes of a secret meeting of Jewish "wise men" held in 1897 to plot the overthrow of civilization. It's been described by many historians as a document of immense power, a "warrant for genocide," inspiring Hitler to carry out the extermination of six million Jews in what he called "the final solution of the Jewish problem in Europe." It's been translated into many languages, reprinted many times, and it's sold millions of copies.

Imaginary Global Community

And yet, it's a very strange document, a confused jumble of ideas that contains none of the traditional features of religious anti-Semitism, such as the fantastical and absurd "blood libel," involving allegations of the murder of Christian boys by Jews for supposed ritual purposes.

Nor did the Protocols exhibit any of the features of the new, racist anti-Semitism that was just surfacing at the time. They showed an imaginary global community of Jews, bound together by religion, plotting to destroy the old European order through liberalism and socialism, Freemasonry and big industry, financial speculation and the arms race (a sign of the document's composition not long before the first World War).

By the time the document, originally composed in Russian, was translated and popularised after 1918, it was already out of date. And in 1920 it was revealed by the London *Times* to be a concoction of paragraphs lifted from a mid-19th-century French satire and a German Gothic novel, with elements added by its Russian compiler. It was not a genuine set of minutes of Jewish conspirators at all. The fact that it was a falsification was confirmed in a major trial held in Berne, Switzerland, in 1934-1935.

And yet, this did little to discredit it in the eyes of anti-Semites. The contents of the document were less important than its claim to provide authentic evidence of the Jewish world conspiracy emanating from the Jewish community itself. For Hitler, writing in his autobiographical tract, *Mein Kampf*, the Protocols exposed "consciously" "what many Jews do unconsciously."

As Nazi propaganda minister Joseph Goebbels wrote in his diary in 1943: "One can't speak of a conspiracy of the Jewish race in any straightforward meaning of the term; this conspiracy is more a characteristic of the race than a case of intellectual intentions. The Jews will always act as their Jewish instinct tells them." It didn't matter, he went on, whether the Protocols were genuine or not, because they exposed a deeper truth about the Jewish racial character.

George Soros

The Protocols did not invent the idea of a Jewish world conspiracy—it was around long before they were concocted; all they did was supposedly confirm it. And the idea has survived in various forms to the present day. It can be seen for example in the self-styled QAnon conspiracy theorists, who believe that a secret cabal of leading Democrats, liberals and Hollywood actors is kidnapping children and subjecting them to various forms of abuse, including the extraction of adrenaline from their bodies—an obvious rehash of the medieval "blood libel."

Behind this, some of them believe, is the Rothschild Jewish banking dynasty, aided and abetted by the Hungarian-American international financier George Soros, also Jewish. Such beliefs have real consequences: QAnon followers were prominent for example in the mob that stormed the Capitol building in Washington DC on January 6th. Anti-Semitism emerged at a violent "Unite the Right" rally in Charlottesville, Virginia, in 2017, as part of the "Great Replacement Theory," a belief according to which the white race in America is being driven out by racial minorities: the demonstrators also chanted "Jews will not replace us!"

Anti-Semitism is a key component in anti-vaccine groups. A study of 27 of them found anti-Semitic conspiracy theories in 79 per cent, from paranoid fantasies of a Jewish plot to destroy the economy by spreading the virus, to using the vaccine to destroy the fertility of the "white race."

None of this is harmless. Quite apart from encouraging people who believe in such ideas not to be vaccinated, making them a danger to others as well as to themselves, it also stokes racial prejudice against Jews, leading to many kinds of discrimination, hate speech and acts of violence.

Social media companies are beginning to confront the spread of the hatred and misinformation. But there is a long way to go. Free speech necessarily has its limits: currently, however, we seem uncertain about where those limits lie. We need to decide before it is too late.

> *"What I hadn't anticipated was the media's reaction to Trump's sudden embrace of birtherism—the degree to which the line between news and entertainment had become so blurred."*

Donald Trump's Birtherism Theory About Barack Obama Opened the Door to a New Wave of Conspiracies

Ted Johnson

In the following viewpoint, Ted Johnson recounts the birtherism conspiracy primarily peddled by Donald Trump early on in Barack Obama's presidency. In 2011, Trump alleged that Obama had not been born in the United States and therefore would be ineligible to be president—the US Constitution states that the president must be a "natural born citizen." The attention given to Trump by the media led to not only Obama releasing his long-form birth certificate as proof of his natural-born citizenship, but also in 2011 brutally taking down Trump at the White House Correspondents' Association dinner, a moment most commonly connected to Trump's decision to run for president in the following election cycle. Ted Johnson is a Washington, DC-based journalist who covers politics, media, and entertainment.

"Barack Obama Recounts Ribbing Donald Trump at White House Correspondents' Dinner—and Why the Mockery Didn't Matter: 'He in Fact Had Never Been Bigger,'" by Ted Johnson, Deadline Hollywood, November 17, 2020. Reprinted by permission.

As you read, consider the following questions:

1. How was Donald Trump's birtherism conspiracy legitimized by the media during President Barack Obama's presidency, and how did that open the door for legitimization of future conspiracies like QAnon?
2. What standards can media, both traditional and online, use to inform the public on the difference between fact and fiction?
3. What could the traditional media have done to squash the inaccurate birtherism myth perpetuated by Donald Trump prior to his election as president?

Barack Obama is on a publicity blitz for his new memoir *A Promised Land*, and he's already drawn headlines for his warnings about democracy in the face of rampant disinformation in the media.

He does go into some detail about how he himself countered Donald Trump's false suggestion that Obama was not born in the United States. Trump drew loads of media attention in 2011 as he pursued the birther lie, compelling Obama to ultimately produce his long-form birth certificate.

In his memoir, Obama describes what happened next: Appearing at the White House Correspondents' Association dinner that year, he unleashed a brutal takedown of Trump, who was then teasing the idea of a presidential run.

"Fortunately it turned out that the country's leading distraction had been invited to sit at the *Washington Post*'s table that night, and those of us aware of what was going on took odd comfort in knowing that once Donald Trump entered the room, it was all but guaranteed that the media would not be thinking about Pakistan," Obama writes.

That was a reference to what was going on in secret at the time: Plans for a raid to take out Osama bin Laden, with US intelligence having been tipped to his whereabouts in Pakistan.

Obama writes that he went to the dinner that night, "my face fixed in an accommodating smile, as I quietly balanced on a mental high wire, my thoughts thousands of miles away."

"When it was my turn to speak, I stood up and started my routine. About halfway through, I turned my attention directly to Trump," he writes.

Obama needled Trump over the birth certificate matter, but also mocked him for *Celebrity Apprentice*.

Obama writes, "As the audience broke into laughter, I continued in this vein, noting his 'credentials and breadth of experience' as host of *Celebrity Apprentice* and congratulating him for how he'd handled the fact that 'at the steakhouse, the men's cooking team did not impress the judges from Omaha Steaks....These are the kinds of decisions that would keep me up at night. Well handled, sir. Well handled.'"

He went on, "The audience howled as Trump sat in silence, cracking a tepid smile. I couldn't begin to guess what went through his mind during the few minutes I spent publicly ribbing him. What I knew was that he was a spectacle, and in the United States of America in 2011, that was a form of power. Trump trafficked in a currency that, however shallow, seemed to gain more purchase with each passing day. The same reporters who laughed at my jokes would continue to give him airtime. Their publishers would vie to have him sit at their tables. Far from being ostracized for the conspiracies he'd peddled, he in fact had never been bigger."

Promised Land is just part one of the Obama memoirs, as it goes through the death of bin Laden. But Obama still devotes a number of passages to Trump's rise as a national political figure, and makes it clear the extent to which he believes that the *Celebrity Apprentice* host was aided and abetted by a political environment where entertainment and politics have linked.

"What I hadn't anticipated was the media's reaction to Trump's sudden embrace of birtherism—the degree to which the line between news and entertainment had become so blurred, and the competition for ratings so fierce, that outlets eagerly lined up to offer a platform for a baseless claim," Obama writes, adding that it was not just Fox News that gave Trump a platform but ABC's *The View* and CNN. He also singled out NBC's *Today*, "the same network that aired Trump's reality show *The Celebrity Apprentice* in prime time and that clearly didn't mind the extra publicity its star was generating."

"Outside the Fox universe, I couldn't say that any mainstream journalists explicitly gave credence to these bizarre charges. They all made a point of expressing polite incredulity, asking Trump, for example, why he thought George Bush and Bill Clinton had never been asked to produce their birth certificates. (He'd usually reply with something along the lines of 'Well, we know they were born in this country.') But at no point did they simply and forthrightly call Trump out for lying or state that the conspiracy theory he was promoting was racist. Certainly, they made little to no effort to categorize his theories as beyond the pale—like alien abduction or the anti-Semitic conspiracies in the Protocols of the Elders of Zion. And the more oxygen the media gave them, the more newsworthy they appeared."

Obama does make reference to the way that he drew on celebrity figures to help propel his rise, including Oprah Winfrey, and how his White House embraced showbiz talent, with the likes of Paul McCartney and Bob Dylan performing as part of a regular PBS concert series. And in promoting the book, Obama will sit down with Winfrey, Jimmy Kimmel and Stephen Colbert, among others.

He does connect Trump's spreading of conspiracy theories to Mitch McConnell and John Boehner's distortions of Obama-era policies, but "the only difference between Trump's style of politics and theirs was Trump's lack of inhibition."

Obama writes, "While I doubted that he was willing to relinquish his business holdings or subject himself to the necessary vetting in order to run for president, I knew that the passions he was tapping, the dark, alternative vision he was promoting and legitimizing, were something I'd likely be contending with for the remainder of my presidency."

In his interviews promoting *Promised Land*, Obama has suggested that the media environment has only worsened since he left office, particularly with the growing power of social media giants like Facebook and Twitter. On *60 Minutes*, Obama suggested that one of the solutions to the current polarization—fueled by a failure to even agree on a common set of facts—lies at the local level.

"I think we're going to have to work with the media and with the tech companies to find ways to inform the public better about the issues and to bolster the standards that ensure we can separate truth from fiction," he said.

He added, "I am somebody who does not blame the current partisanship solely on Donald Trump or solely on social media. You already saw some of these trends taking place early in my presidency. But I do think they've kept on getting worse."

Viewpoint 

> *"The belief that the people of the Middle Ages thought the Earth was flat and were re-educated by Christopher Columbus is an example of the widespread myth that medieval people were either stupid, ignorant, or both."*

Why Has the Flat Earth Theory Persisted?

Shiloh Carroll

In the following viewpoint, Shiloh Carroll demystifies one of the most well-known conspiracy theories in history: that Earth is flat. The author details how, in spite of the myths that people of medieval times believed Earth was flat, it was actually well known that Earth is a sphere. Carroll goes on to detail how—incredibly—the flat-Earth beliefs have grown with the advent of the internet, which allows for the easy spread of information and scientific knowledge but also the spread of misinformation, especially in conspiracy-prone echo chambers. Shiloh Carroll is a PhD who works in the writing center at Tennessee State University. She is the author of Medievalism in A Song of Ice and Fire and Game of Thrones.

"Getting to the Bottom of the Flat Earth," by Shiloh Carroll, *The Public Medievalist*, June 13, 2019. Reprinted by permission.

As you read, consider the following questions:

1. What is Poe's law and why does it explain how the flat-Earth myth has persisted for centuries and has grown further with the invention of the internet?
2. How and why did the religions of the eighteenth and nineteenth centuries perpetuate the myth that Earth is flat?
3. How has the internet given further rise to the belief that Earth is flat, in spite of all the science backing the understanding that Earth is a sphere?

In fourteen-hundred and ninety-two, Columbus sailed the ocean blue—and discovered that the Earth, despite the beliefs of the Catholic Church and Spanish royalty—was round.

Right?

Absolutely. Not.

People—ancient and medieval—have known the Earth is spherical since at least the 6th century BCE. Ancient Greek mathematician Pythagoras was likely the first to propose the idea, though his argument was based on philosophy and aesthetics rather than mathematics and astronomy. But physical evidence that the earth was round followed, thanks in part to Aristotle and Eratosthenes. The knowledge was not lost with the end of the Western Roman Empire, either. In *The Reckoning of Time*, Bede (who lived circa CE 673-735) refers to the Earth as an "orb" and says that "it is not merely circular like a shield or spread out like a wheel, but resembles more a ball." This idea was repeated by philosophers, mathematicians, and astronomers throughout the Middle Ages.

And yet, the idea that medieval people believed in a flat Earth is one of those maddeningly tenacious pieces of "common knowledge." It's one of those pieces of knowledge trotted out when people want to claim how "stupid" or "backward" medieval people were.

Fast forward to the present, and everything old is new again. There are a surprising number of people—who generally call themselves "flat-earthers"—who promote the belief that the world is flat. *The Guardian* recently released a short documentary video about them. Netflix has a feature-length documentary. This profoundly retro conspiracy theory has particularly found a home on the internet, where it has been notoriously promoted by popular YouTube stars like Logan Paul.

While it's possible some of these modern flat-Earthers may think they're carrying on a tradition from the Middle Ages, their beliefs actually originated in the 1830s. And not at all coincidentally, that is roughly the same time that the myth that medieval people thought the world was flat was born, as well.

The Round Earth Rebellion That Never Was

These ideas and their history have been extensively debunked by Jeffrey Burton Russell in his excellent book *Inventing the Flat Earth*. The belief that the people of the Middle Ages thought the Earth was flat and were re-educated by Christopher Columbus is an example of the widespread myth that medieval people were either stupid, ignorant, or both. But if you look under the hood of this notion, it actually says less about the Middle Ages than it does about the people who championed the idea. Take 19th century French philosopher Auguste Comte, whose theory of positivism says that human intellectual and social development happened in a straight line from Neanderthal to his own image of a refined gentleman. Claims like this fundamentally, and in some cases purposefully, misunderstand the historical record so that the perpetrators can feel superior to the past—and were often used to justify racism, colonialism, and imperialism.

Medieval intellectuals knew very well that the Earth is a sphere. Medieval philosophers and theologians had access to the Greek and Arabic works of "natural philosophy" (a.k.a. "science") in Latin translations. Bede, for example, demonstrated that the changing length of daylight in different seasons was due to the sphericity of the Earth. Roger Bacon (c. 1219-1292 CE) argued that the Earth is spherical and that other lands on the opposite side of the globe existed and could be visited. Scientists discussed the rotation of the Earth and the other planets, and while they did believe that the Earth was the center of the universe, they believed the universe itself was spherical. Even the author of *Mandeville's Travels*, who believed in (or at least wrote about) people with giant feet to shade their heads, wrote about a spherical Earth, time zones, and people not falling off the other side of the planet.

With all the evidence that medieval scholars knew that the Earth is round, where did we get the idea that they believed the Earth was flat? The core of the idea can be traced back to 18th– and 19th-century progressivists, who decided that science and religion—that religion specifically being Roman Catholicism—had always been at war. John William Draper, for example, argued that religion was based on magic and thus antithetical to science; he also blamed St. Augustine in particular for turning the Bible from a model for a moral life into "the arbiter of human knowledge, an audacious tyranny over the mind of man."

Historians such as William Whewell and Andrew Dickson White argued that Catholicism was inherently opposed to progress; creating an ignorant medieval world allowed eighteenth- and nineteenth-century Protestant thinkers to put down the Catholicism of their day. Historians and biographers cherry-picked their "medieval" sources. They insisted that people like Cosmas (who wrote in CE 500s, at the very beginning of the Middle Ages) and Lactantius (who wrote around CE 250-375, well before the Middle Ages), who did argue for a flat Earth model, were much more influential than they actually were. They also pointed to maps by people such as Isidore of Seville and Saint Augustine—maps that were spiritual or conceptual descriptions of the world and not practical navigational maps—claiming that 15th-century navigators relied on these maps to sail. Those maps were part of religious texts, and would have only ever seen a ship if they were being carefully transported in a monk's belongings!

For other nineteenth-century writers, the medieval flat-Earther myth was part of a nationalist project, one that painted Christopher Columbus as a scrappy, rebellious hero rather than the genocidal asshole he really was.

American writer and historian Washington Irving was one of the first to promote this myth. He wrote *A History of the Life and Voyages of Christopher Columbus* in 1828—a book which freely mixed fact and fiction to create a "Hero Columbus," beset by naysayers of every type, fighting against "errors and prejudices, the mingled ignorance and erudition, and the pedantic bigotry" of everybody who wasn't him. Similarly Antoine-Jean Letronne, an intellectual prodigy from France, claimed that medieval people who knew the Earth was round were "outliers" and that the Catholic Church "forced" people to believe in a Biblically-mandated flat Earth.

The public believed these men because they were eminent scholars. But they built their body of knowledge about the beliefs of the medieval people by citing each other; intellectual echo-chambers are nothing new.

Why were scholars so eager to buy into the lie that medieval people thought the Earth was flat? It comes down to the same needs behind many of the erroneous beliefs about the Middle Ages: modern people need somewhere to put ignorance, backwardness, and barbarism. They need to feel superior to someone else. The Middle Ages is, very often, where that need ends up. "Flat Earther" is a useful shorthand for willful ignorance, usually used as code for people who refuse to accept modern science, or a slightly-more polite way of calling someone "barbarian."

But that raises another question: what has caused a group of people today—who have access to much more advanced science including photographs of the spherical earth—to insist that the Earth is flat? Why do they insist upon the idea that the spherical Earth is a conspiracy perpetrated on humankind by scientists, governments, and "deep state operatives" for the last 3,000 years?

Flat Earth Utopia

The modern argument really started with nineteenth-century Englishman Samuel Birley Rowbotham. Rowbotham wrote a pamphlet in the 1830s that he called *Zetetic Astronomy: Earth Not a Globe* under the pseudonym "Parallax." This was first published in 1849, and expanded into a book in 1865.

In it, Parallax argues for a Christian Fundamentalist, biblically literal interpretation of the world—that the Earth is flat, was created in six literal days, is only 6,000 years old, and is headed rapidly toward the apocalypse. His conception of the Earth was that it is a flat disc with the North Pole at the center and a massive ice wall around the outside edge.

He did not say anything about whether there were White Walkers on the other side, so let's assume not.

Rowbotham came up with some very complicated projections to explain the cycles of night and day, the seasons, and eclipses. But central to his thesis was his attack on the scientific method, which he claimed "take[s] the liberty of inventing certain principles and hypotheses" and then creating mathematical models to prove those hypotheses.

The scientific method absolutely does not work this way. But that is the straw-man that he argues against.

Instead, he argued for logic and observation—"that natural and legitimate mode of investigation." At the end of his pamphlet, he argues that Newtonian theory is "a prolific source of irreligion and atheism" and he argues that to reject the Biblical model of the Earth as flat is to reject all Biblical teachings. He certainly knew how to stake out an extreme position.

Since then, the flat-Earth belief has followed both a Biblical literalism and an anti-modern-science thread, not always at the same time by the same people. If you're interested in how the belief propagated down through the generations and the people who pushed it, Christine Garwood's book *Flat Earth: The History of an Infamous Idea* provides a deep dive into it, but here's a brief summary:

Rowbotham's followers (who eventually established the Universal Zetetic Society in 1893) did a bunch of stunts trying to get people to prove the Earth is spherical while rejecting every bit of evidence anybody brought forward. For example, in 1870, John Hampden offered a cash reward for proof that the Earth was spherical. Alfred Russell Wallace took him up on it.

Fun fact: Wallace devised his own theory of evolution from natural selection that was published at the same time as Darwin's; Wallace was no scientific slouch.

Wallace set up a very basic experiment—three sticks in a line along a canal between two bridges—to show the drop in elevation due to the curvature of the Earth. According to Wallace, Carpenter declared that "the fact that the distant signal appeared below the middle one as far as the middle one did below the cross-hair, proved that the three were in a straight line, and that the earth was flat." The experiment, of course, showed the exact opposite, but Carpenter was not one to let evidence get in the way.

Across the pond, in 1899, preacher and faith-healer John Alexander Dowie established the town of Zion, Illinois, as a Christian utopia; it became the major center of American flat-Earth belief. Unfortunately for Zion, Dowie was greedy and vastly narcissistic. He declared himself the reincarnation of the prophet Elijah and bankrupted the town so he could live in luxury. Ultimately, the people of Zion rejected Dowie's teachings and voted to become secular.

Samuel Shenton established the International Flat Earth Research Society in 1956 and spent his life trying to prove that the space program was faked—and also, somehow, that the space program actually proved the Earth is flat. His successor, Charles Kenneth Johnson, brought the conspiracy theories.

- He claimed that Columbus had discovered the Earth was flat, not round, on his voyage.
- He claimed that Satan had convinced Copernicus that the Earth was a sphere.

- He claimed that NASA continued the lie about the Earth being a sphere because it created jobs.
- He claimed that prominent science fiction author Arthur C. Clarke wrote and directed the moon landing.
- He claimed that the moon landing was shot in Meteor Crater in Arizona.
- He claimed that the *Challenger* disaster was either a plot by NASA to cover up that they couldn't actually leave the atmosphere or God's divine judgment for trying.
- He even claimed that O.J. Simpson's role in 1977 film *Capricorn One* (about a faked Mars landing) is the reason he was "framed" for murder.
- This is apparently why O.J. Simpson was allegedly "framed" for murder. You heard it here first, folks.

None of these claims are true. Many are provably false. But that does not matter in the mind of a conspiracy theorist like Johnson.

All of these people had different reasons for believing in—or pretending to believe in—a flat Earth. Some were religious, some were concerned about government overreach, and some were flat-out cons. But their beliefs spread and persisted, undeterred by science or evidence.

Wired Flat-Earthers

In the 21st century, flat-Earth belief has grown. But at the same time, it has grown even more perplexing. Partially this is because of the rise of the Internet. The Internet allows for an unprecedented ability to spread information and scientific knowledge. But on the flip side, this same function allows the spread of misinformation and self-curated echo chambers where conspiracy theories flourish.

Poe's Law helps us understand why. Poe's Law is a theory of Internet culture identified by Nathan Poe in 2005, where he stated: "Without a winking smiley or other blatant display of humor, it is utterly impossible to parody a Creationist in such a way that someone won't mistake for the genuine article. [sic]"

Today, this is often generalized to say that any satire of any extreme position is indistinguishable from sincere belief in that position. So, it is nearly impossible to tell which of the people on the many websites, forums, Facebook groups, and conferences devoted to belief in a Flat Earth are true believers, and which ones are "just trolling." Likewise, some other proposed beliefs among these people, such as that there is "no such thing as forests," seem so outlandish that most people won't be able to understand how believers could possibly reach these conclusions.

Flat-Eartherism is so mixed up with other conspiracy theories that it can be difficult not to dismiss these people as kooks and ignore them. But their beliefs—those of them who truly believe it—are a symptom of a larger societal problem and also a function of human psychology. Some of it, especially the strain passed down by Rowbotham, is anti-intellectualist. Broadly speaking, people tend to like understanding things, and dislike being unable to understand them. When they find new information challenging, many choose instead to fall back on a predetermined worldview or simply believe their own senses—even when those senses are incapable of perceiving something like the size of the globe. So when scientists tell them their senses are wrong or inadequate, they'll push back.

The other strain is conspiracy belief, which has its own set of psychological indicators, but is tied up in the human brain's tendency to find patterns where there are none (part of what psychologists call the "conjunctive fallacy"). As we can see from the list of theories Johnson introduced to the flat-Earth idea, conspiracy theories tend to travel in packs and are highly political in nature. But they require social interaction to thrive, which the Internet has provided in spades. Conspiracy belief also correlates with feelings of isolation, powerlessness, and overactive pattern-finding.

Essentially, conspiracy theories give people a sense of control over an uncontrollable world, or at least a reason why they can't control it—because "the deep state" or a "one-world government" or the Illuminati (or all of the above) is actively working against them and people like them. The flat Earth conspiracy, in particular, encourages people both to believe their own senses over science, and to think the government is hiding something out beyond the "ice wall" that is Antarctica. They want to have their conspiratorial cake and eat it too.

A Fundamentally Modern Flat Earth

What is truly remarkable is the medieval flat Earth myth and modern conspiracy theories actually have no history in common. Modern flat-Earthers are not carrying on a belief system from the Middle Ages. They do not, for the most part, even claim that they are. Yet both uses of the flat Earth theory are ways for people to feel superior to others. If medieval people thought the Earth was flat, we (who do not believe such silly things) can show how much more developed and intelligent we are than them.

On the flip side, believing in the conspiracy is like betting on a huge long-shot to win a horse race. Sure, it may be risky. But imagine the mental rewards if you win: if all of science is proven wrong, and NASA et al. are found to have been lying to us for 3,000 years, then the flat Earth conspiracy believers can claim to be so much smarter than everyone else. That's why they use every intellectual trick in the book to call the "race" in their favor; they've bet their reputation, and even their identity, on a ridiculous long shot. They need to win.

In either case there are innate human needs to be right, and to feel better than others. This need feeds both of these beliefs—the belief that we are better than medieval people, and that the earth is flat. Ultimately these needs can lead people to believe the unbelievable in their quest for superiority.

It can be tempting to blame the Internet for conspiracy beliefs. It's tempting to want to burn the whole Internet to the ground. But conspiracies have been around for as long as humankind has. Research has shown that laughing at people who cling to conspiracies only makes them cling harder. As with so many things, prevention is the best way to combat conspiracy belief; psychologists have found that presenting scientific research to people before they're exposed to conspiracy theories is key to helping them to not fall for these theories. Education is vitally important, both for teaching facts, for developing critical thinking abilities, and for preventing the spread of the dangerous misinformation running wild on the internet.

So, at the risk of ruthless self-promotion, make sure to share this article, and others on this subject, with everyone you know. It might be the only thing standing between them and building a homemade, steam-powered rocket in hopes of proving the Earth is really flat.

> *"The area is like a gathering station where they capture people, ships and aircraft to conduct research."*

The Mystery of the Bermuda Triangle Lends Itself to Conspiracy Theories

The Week

In the following viewpoint, the staff of The Week *shares six conspiracy theories about the mystery of the Bermuda Triangle, a region in the western part of the North Atlantic Ocean near the British island territory, where a number of aircraft and ships are said to have disappeared under mysterious circumstances. The authors detail six attempts at explanations for the disappearances—there is an average of 4 planes and 20 boats that disappear in the region each year—from potentially science-based explanations to the more outlandish ideas like aliens or the lost island of Atlantis.* The Week *is a weekly news magazine with British and US editions.*

As you read, consider the following questions:

1. Could the disappearances inside the Bermuda Triangle be caused by rogue waves?
2. Why are Bermuda Triangle conspiracies so popular?
3. Will there ever be a widely accepted explanation for the disappearances inside the Bermuda Triangle?

"Bermuda Triangle: Six Conspiracy Theories About the Mystery," *The Week*, April 10, 2019. Reprinted by permission.

The mystery of the Bermuda Triangle, a patch of ocean which has supposedly caused the demise of countless ships and planes that have passed through it, has puzzled scientists for years.

The Triangle is an area of the North Atlantic ocean between Bermuda to the north, Puerto Rico to the south and Florida to the west. An average of four planes and 20 boats are said to vanish in the zone every year, leaving no trace behind.

As the *Daily Mail* says: "From sub-sea pyramids to hexagonal clouds and alien bases, scientists and conspiracy theorist alike have drummed up every imaginable scenario over the years to explain the mysterious disappearances in the Bermuda Triangle."

However, one scientist has suggested a new theory that may solve the mystery once and for all—rogue waves.

Here are six theories behind the science of the Bermuda Triangle:

Rogue Waves

According to Channel 5 documentary *The Bermuda Triangle Enigma*, scientists now believe conditions in that area are just right for "massive rogue waves," and have used simulators to demonstrate how these could put ships at risk.

"There are storms to the south and north, which come together," said University of Southampton oceanographer Simon Boxall. "And if there are additional ones from Florida, it can be a potentially deadly formation of rogue waves."

The Huffington Post reports that rogue waves of this type of wave could reach 100ft tall, which would be on par with the largest wave ever recorded, a "100-foot tsunami triggered by an earthquake and landslide in Alaska's Lituya Bay in 1958."

Magnetic Forces Causing Compass Malfunctions

The Bermuda Triangle is one of two places on earth where compasses point to true north (the geographic North Pole) rather than magnetic north (the shifting magnetic North Pole), says How Stuff Works.

Reasonable Explanations

A history of speculation surrounds the area west of Florida, south of Puerto Rico, and north of Bermuda called the Bermuda Triangle. The Bermuda Triangle is the area that over 50 ships and dozens of planes have disappeared. Multiple theories have formulated to explain this phenomenon, the first being the "Methane Gas Theory." Some scientists have claimed the reason ships and planes disappear is that of the methane gas and oil deposits found at the bottom of the sea. The mass of the gas and oil can cause large eruptions that burst through the surface. Another theory claims the disappearances are due to no more than "rogue waves." Oceanographer Simon Boxall of University of Southampton claimed the reason there are no traces of the missing ships and planes because "there are storms to the south and north which come together and additional ones that come from Florida." In addition to the "Rogue Wave Theory," there is the "Sargasso Sea Theory." The Sargasso Sea is the area within the Bermuda Triangle where ocean currents meet to bind the certain spot and could trap ships that pass through as it causes them to stop moving. As there are many more theories ranging from practical to supernatural, there are contrasting theories that use more rationale to explain the Bermuda Triangle disappearances. Karl Kruszelnicki, an Australian scientist who performed research on the Bermuda Triangle, declared that the missing vessels and planes are nothing but "human error, bad weather, heavy air, and sea traffic." The unconvinced scientists insisted the high rate of ships and planes that went missing was nothing supernatural, just unfortunate circumstances. The US Coastguard was asked to reflect on the disappearances to which they concluded, "The number that go missing in the Bermuda Triangle is about the same as everywhere else in the world." There are logical explanations for the boats and planes to go missing as well as theories regarding alien abduction. Although there are reasonable explanations, many are skeptical about the declarations of Kruszelnicki and the US Coastguard regarding the Bermuda Triangle.

"The Psychology of Extraordinary Beliefs: The Bermuda Triangle," by Affie Siddiqui, The Ohio State University, February 11, 2019.

Some theories have suggested that the agonic line, the point where the magnetic and true north are perfectly aligned, passes through the Bermuda Triangle, resulting in a magnetic phenomenon which could explain cases where pilots and ship captains claimed their compasses ceased to work properly, causing them to veer off-course.

The problem with this theory is that early 18th century scientists discovered that the agonic line shifts each year. While it did pass through the Bermuda Triangle at one point, it now goes through the Gulf of Mexico instead.

Methane Bubbles

A series of huge craters discovered on the seabed around the coast of Norway in 2016 may also give scientists vital information in solving the mystery.

The craters measure up to half-a-mile wide and are 150ft deep, and are believed to have been formed by bubbles of largely methane gas leaking from deposits of oil and gas buried deep in the sea floor. Once these gasses reach a critical mass before bursting to the surface, they can cause large eruptions.

Atlantis

One of the more outlandish conspiracy theories centres around the Bermuda Triangle actually being the location of the mythical Lost City of Atlantis.

The Independent recounts one blog poster who explained: "When Atlantis was destroyed it sank to the very bottom of the ocean.

"While the ruined temples now play host to multitudinous underwater creatures, the great Atlantean fire-crystals that once provided so much of the tremendous power and energy that was found in Atlantis still exist."

Aliens

The Sun explains that some writers "have blamed UFOs for the disappearances," and that they "believe that aliens use the Triangle as a portal to travel to and from our planet."

"The area is like a gathering station where they capture people, ships and aircraft to conduct research."

No Mystery

Last year Australian scientist Karl Kruszelnicki claimed that the high number of disappearances cannot be explained by aliens or Atlantis, or even by the more plausible theories involving rogue waves.

Instead, he suggests that the "mystery" is nothing more than a perfect mix of human error, bad weather and a high concentration of ships in the area.

"It is close to the Equator, near a wealthy part of the world—America—therefore you have a lot of traffic," he told *The Independent* last year.

"According to Lloyd's of London and the US Coastguard, the number that go missing in the Bermuda Triangle is the same as anywhere in the world on a percentage basis."

Viewpoint 6

> *"The Illuminati has existed since the dawn of time. Its insignia can be seen on the pyramids, its influence was evident around the life of Christ, and their top bananas—such as for example the Queen—are in fact ancient lizards dating from an era before man existed."*

What in the World Is the Illuminati?

Martha Gill

In the following viewpoint, Martha Gill takes a tongue-in-cheek approach to examine the vast history of the Illuminati conspiracy theory. An organization that has (maybe) existed since the dawn of time, the Illuminati can be found everywhere, including the pyramids in Egypt, or traced to 1776 when a man named Adam Weishaupt couldn't afford to be admitted into the Freemasons and created his own order. The group, which according to the conspiracy aims to establish a new world order, would create a place where nation states would be banished. According to a poll released in 2013, 28 percent of US voters believe in the existence of the Illuminati. Martha Gill is a columnist at the New Statesman, *where she writes about politics, culture, and neuroscience.*

"What Is the Illuminati? You Asked Google—Here's the Answer," by Martha Gill, Guardian News and Media Limited, November 22, 2017. Reprinted by permission.

As you read, consider the following questions:

1. How did attempts to show people the dangers of fake news in the 1960s backfire and lead to further belief into the Illuminati conspiracy?
2. What, if any, are the drawbacks of popular figures like Katy Perry, Madonna, and Rihanna perpetuating the myth of the Illuminati, and how can it potentially lead their fans toward further and more radicalized conspiracy theories?
3. How is the broadness of the Illuminati conspiracy theory similar to the broadness of the QAnon conspiracy theory? How is it different?

You shouldn't have Googled that, you're on a list now. And I really hope you didn't read anything that came up. Knowing anything at all about the Illuminati is very risky—first because they will suspect you are on to them and track you down ruthlessly, and second because you could accidentally end up mentioning some of these facts in conversation, meaning you will never be taken seriously ever again.

So it is at great personal risk and solely to protect you, the reader, that I will try to complete this article leaving you entirely "knowledge neutral." Here is everything you need:

What Is the Illuminati?

It is a powerful and savagely guarded organisation that secretly controls the entire modern world, probably while wearing cloaks. It has done this mainly through infiltrating the media and brainwashing everybody. It could be doing it right now.

Alternately, it is one of the world's most persistent conspiracy theories. Persistent because, unlike the piffling conspiracy theories on the 1969 moon landings, John F. Kennedy's assassination, and 9/11, which limit themselves with regard to space and time, Illuminati enthusiasts believe that something is up with everything ever, which as it turns out is very hard to disprove.

When Was It Founded?

The Illuminati has existed since the dawn of time. Its insignia can be seen on the pyramids, its influence was evident around the life of Christ, and their top bananas—such as for example the Queen—are in fact ancient lizards dating from an era before man existed (a belief that often comes with some rather unpleasant antisemitic underpinnings). Alternately, it was founded in Bavaria on 1 May 1776, by a man called Adam Weishaupt, who couldn't afford the Freemason admission fee. His society—The Order of the Illuminati—grew from five members to thousands in just a few years, but then, after Karl Theodor became ruler of Bavaria, secret societies were made punishable by death, and there the order ended.

What Is It Trying to Do?

It wants nothing less than to establish a new world order over which an authoritarian gang of elites would rule, and under which nation states would be banished. Alternately, it is part of a fight against fake news, which began in the 1960s. A journalist for *Playboy* magazine called Robert Anton Wilson, along with a writer called Kerry Thornley, who had written a jokey text on the Illuminati, decided that the world was becoming too authoritarian, and one way to shake that up would be to get people to start questioning what they read.

They started sending in fake letters from readers talking about a secret organisation called the Illuminati. They would then send in more letters, contradicting these claims. They hoped that these contrary points of view would get people to view the news a little more sceptically. Instead everyone just got very excited about the Illuminati, and the myth spread worldwide.

Who Is in the Illuminati?

Katy Perry, Beyoncé, Jay Z, Madonna, Kim Kardashian, Lady Gaga, Rihanna. Yes, the music industry in fact controls the planet, via, we must assume, the rise of free music-streaming services, which are rapidly causing their own demise. It's a very clever cover-up.

Alternately, none of these people are in the Illuminati, because, rather than sending hooded figures to deal with pesky internet writers who put it about, they deliberately encourage the rumours. Madonna, for example, released a single titled "Illuminati," claiming in an interview with *Rolling Stone* that she knew who the "real Illuminati" were. Beyoncé puts references in her lyrics (In "Formation": "Y'all haters corny with that Illuminati mess"), and Katy Perry once admitted she believed in aliens. Or maybe they're double bluffing.

How Many People Believe in the Illuminati?

According to a 2013 poll of US voters by Public Policy Polling (a Democrat-leaning polling firm), 28%. Something to ponder.

Periodical and Internet Sources Bibliography

The following articles have been selected to supplement the diverse views presented in this chapter.

Danielle Abril, "The Biggest Conspiracy Theories of 2020 (and Why They Won't Die)," *Fortune*, December 30, 2020. https://fortune.com/2020/12/30/2020-conspiracy-theories-presidential-election-covid-19-coronavirus-qanon/

Zack Beauchamp, "Marjorie Taylor Greene's Space Laser and the Age-Old Problem of Blaming the Jews," Vox, January 30, 2021. https://www.vox.com/22256258/marjorie-taylor-greene-jewish-space-laser-anti-semitism-conspiracy-theories

Mark R. Cheathem, "Conspiracy Theories Abounded in 19th-Century American Politics," *Smithsonian*, April 11, 2019. https://www.smithsonianmag.com/history/conspiracy-theories-abounded-19th-century-american-politics-180971940/

Aaron Earls, "Christians, Conspiracy Theories, and Credibility: Why Our Words Today Matter for Eternity," Lifeway Research, February 1, 2021. https://lifewayresearch.com/2021/02/01/christians-conspiracy-theories-and-credibility-why-our-words-today-matter-for-eternity/

Rachel E. Greenspan, "QAnon Builds On Centuries of Anti-Semitic Conspiracy Theories That Put Jewish People at Risk," *Insider*, October 24, 2020. https://www.insider.com/qanon-conspiracy-theory-anti-semitism-jewish-racist-believe-save-children-2020-10

Mya Jaradat, "Why Would Christians Embrace Conspiracy Theories?" *Deseret News*, March 28, 2021. https://www.deseret.com/indepth/2021/3/28/22334183/what-group-of-christians-most-likely-believe-conspiracy-theories-white-evangelicals-qanon-faith

Joel Lawrence, "Faith, Apocalypse, and Nationalism: Why Evangelicals Are Vulnerable to Conspiracy Theories," Center for Pastor Theologians, January 25, 2021. https://www.pastortheologians.com/articles/2021/1/25/faith-apocalypse-and

-nationalism-why-evangelicals-are-vulnerable-to-conspiracy-theories

Steve Mirsky, "Flat Earthers: What They Believe and Why," *Scientific American*, March 27, 2020. https://www.scientificamerican.com/podcast/episode/flat-earthers-what-they-believe-and-why/

Shannon Serpette, "Top 7 Theories Behind the Mysterious Bermuda Triangle," 30a, October 30, 2019. https://30a.com/bermuda-triangle/

Blake Stilwell, "6 Wild US Government Conspiracy Theories Explained," Military.com, 2021. https://www.military.com/history/6-wild-us-government-conspiracy-theories-explained.html.

Thomas Tarrants, "We Can Reach Conspiracy Theorists for Christ. Here's How." *Christianity Today*, July 1, 2021. https://www.christianitytoday.com/ct/2021/july-web-only/we-can-reach-conspiracy-theorists-for-christ-heres-how.html

Alyssa Weiner, "Global Trends in Conspiracy Theories Linking Jews with Coronavirus," AJC Global Voice, May 1, 2020. https://www.ajc.org/news/global-trends-in-conspiracy-theories-linking-jews-with-coronavirus

Natalie Wolchover, "Are Flat-Earthers Being Serious?" Live Science, May 30, 2017. https://www.livescience.com/24310-flat-earth-belief.html

How Do People Come Back from Conspiracy Theories?

Chapter Preface

How do people come back from believing in conspiracy theories? The following chapter shows how addicting the belief in the QAnon conspiracy theory can be for its adherents. It explores what not to say to people in order to get them away from conspiracies and also what to say that will offer them the most help and support.

Not only are families trying to come back together in a world post-QAnon, but there are also many families that are still being torn apart and feeling the stresses of having close family members who see themselves as "true believers." One viewpoint showcases stories from teenagers who are living closely to family members who believe in QAnon, and with the COVID-19 pandemic, it is even more challenging to try to avoid.

Another viewpoint explores what specifically brought adherents into QAnon, what brought them out, and how they're helping others—including their own family members—to do the same, including using the same platforms that radicalized them toward QAnon in the first place, like Reddit.

Additionally, this chapter shows what is being done to stop the spread of misinformation online by more aggressive moderation by the leaders of major platforms like Facebook and Twitter. Technology like artificial intelligence and machine learning are taking on the task of stopping the spread of unfounded conspiracies in the online space in the hopes that these conspiracy theories will be quashed before they can spread.

In the wake of the 2020 election, many people who work to help people deprogram from cults are getting called for support in a similar avenue: how to get friends and loved ones away from believing in the QAnon conspiracy theory. But one viewpoint author has a strong opinion against deprogramming.

Viewpoint 1

> *"What can motivate a conspiracy theorist to change their thinking are the friendships and relationships they hold dear. If someone wants to change a conspiracy theorist's mind, it's beneficial to find ways to deepen your relationship with them because that's the thing that can encourage them to change."*

Logic and Reason Won't Work Against Conspiracy Theories

Fortesa Latifi

In the following viewpoint, Fortesa Latifi shares the stories of a number of Gen-Zers who were dealing with family members, parents in particular, who believe in the QAnon conspiracy theory. The viewpoint follows the stories of Emily and Mackenzie, two American teenagers, and Yesenia, a twenty-year-old from Costa Rica, who are all attempting to navigate living with parents who are strong believers in QAnon. These stories show how the conspiracy went international in 2020. The author also speaks to experts about what can be done to help loved ones to come back from conspiracies. Fortesa Latifi is a journalist who contributes to Teen Vogue *and* MTV News, *among other publications.*

"QAnon Conspiracy Theories Are Driving Families Apart," by Fortesa Latifi, *Teen Vogue*,

As you read, consider the following questions:

1. According to the viewpoint, why is it not possible to fight conspiracy theories with logic and reason?
2. What additional challenges has the COVID-19 pandemic put on families dealing with loved ones who are adherents of QAnon?
3. What can children do when they have a parent or loved one who is diving deep into conspiracy theories like QAnon?

Like many Gen-Z'ers, 18-year-old Emily doesn't spend much time on Facebook. Recently, though, she started using the social media platform to find a roommate and look for scholarship opportunities. While browsing, she saw her mother's page, which she said was filled with "crackpot theories" revolving around the popular conspiracy theory QAnon. One of the posts falsely claimed to find a satanic symbol within the Democratic National Committee's logo. For a moment, Emily was relieved to see that her mother's friend had pushed back on the idea with a comment—until it became clear that the friend was only commenting to say that all politicians are satanic.

Emily's mother is one of hundreds of thousands of people who have fallen into the QAnon conspiracy universe, in which America is run by Hollywood elites and Democratic politicians who happen to be satanic pedophiles intent on trafficking children and taking over the world. Oh, and, the only person who can stop the takeover? President Donald Trump.

The conspiracy theory has exploded in popularity in the past few months, with GOP congressional candidates openly supporting QAnon and the most powerful man in the country giving credence to Q's ideas, referring to its followers as "people who love our country" and "like me very much." It was striking enough to see the president refuse to disavow such a bizarre conspiracy theory, but his comments are particularly disturbing given that, last year, an FBI bulletin from the Phoenix office named "conspiracy-theory driven domestic extremists" a threat to the security of the country. In the past year, an alleged QAnon believer armed with multiple guns rammed a truck into a gate near Canadian prime minister Justin Trudeau's home and another was arrested on suspicion of plotting a kidnapping.

Emily, who requested her last name be withheld so she could speak candidly, grew up in Kentucky, in a family where it was normal for her father to give her reading material like *48 Liberal Lies About American History*. She says she mostly went along with her parents' views until she was in seventh grade and got into the popular blogging site Tumblr. There she was exposed to different ideas than those she'd grown up with, and she felt herself pulling away from her parents' ideology. Soon there was tension between Emily and her parents if they discussed anything political. On her 18th birthday, her father took away her car keys and phone and left her alone in her room because she said she wanted to vote for Andrew Yang in the primaries.

Emily now watches her mother get sucked deeper and deeper into the world of Q. "I hate it for me and I hate it for her," Emily says. "It's a spiral. A downward spiral."

She tries to reason with her mother, telling her the articles she shares are from nonreputable news sources (or once, even a satirical website), but it hasn't worked. "She gets very defensive, saying I don't know what I'm talking about and that I think she's stupid," Emily says.

As her mother posts QAnon theories on Facebook, Emily gets texts from her friends: "They're like, 'I can't look at your mother's Facebook.' And I'm like, 'I can't look at my mother's Facebook.' I wish my parents had no access to social media."

Emily has since mostly given up on changing her parents' minds, saying it feels like a lost cause. (Facebook announced on October 6 that their Dangerous Organizations Operations team was moving immediately to remove all "Facebook Pages, Groups and Instagram accounts for representing QAnon.")

QAnon in Terms of Game Design

Reed Berkowitz is the director of the Curioser Institute, which explores the structure and psychology of storytelling through interactive experiences—largely using games, particularly with augmented reality. As a professional game designer, he's been fascinated by QAnon, and the ways it seems to have exploited and subverted the tools of interactive gaming with almost frightening efficiency and deliberate intention.

In the piece, Berkowitz talks a lot about apophenia—the psychological tendency to eagerly seek out patterns where none actually exist. This can be a wild card in game design, he explains, because sometimes players will project and ascribe value onto the wrong things, wasting their time on non-existent patterns, and ultimately blaming the designers on their disappointing gaming experience.

"QAnon grows on the wild misinterpretation of random data, presented in a suggestive fashion in a milieu designed to help the users come to the intended misunderstanding. Maybe 'guided

Cynthia Miller-Idriss, a sociology professor at American University who specializes in extremism, said there's a reason Emily feels like she can't get through to her parents. "You can't fight conspiracy theories with logic or reason," Miller-Idriss says. "It's very difficult to get people to come back from. Even talking about the theory can reinforce it."

Miller-Idriss says it's important for children to remember that it's not their job to fix their parents: "It's already hard in a pandemic to maintain childhood. They need to worry about their own growth and development first."

Mackenzie, 15, who also prefers not to give her last name to protect her family's privacy, lives with her dad part-time since her parents' divorce. When she's at his house, he tries to convince her to believe in QAnon. "One thing he keeps saying is, 'Just you wait, crazy stuff is gonna happen, you just wait,'" Mackenzie says. "I apophenia' is a better phrase. Guided because the puppet masters are directly involved in hinting about the desired conclusions. They have pre-seeded the conclusions. They are constantly getting the player lost by pointing out unrelated random events and creating a meaning for them that fits the propaganda message Q is delivering."

Berkowitz also goes into detail about Q as the obligatory plot device character. The entire point of Q is to deliver exposition that makes the player act—not to divulge information, but to create the fictional world of the game. He also explores the psychological impacts of the "Do your own research!" self-fulfulling prophecies—how a few breadcrumbs can lead someone to the right YouTube video, which cryptically alludes to enough things to spark a dopamine fix that mimics a genuine "Eureka!" moment, which is often all it takes to get the player hooked into the game.

It's a fascinating examination of gaming psychology. But also a horrifying look at the efficiency of conspiracy theories like QAnon.

"A Game Designer Explains the Success of QAnon, in Terms of Game Design," by Thom Dunn, Boing Boing, November 19, 2020.

just roll my eyes like, 'Yeah, for sure, Hillary Clinton is gonna get arrested for eating the fetuses Planned Parenthood provides to her.'"

For Mackenzie, the gulf between her and her dad is complex. "I love my dad," she says, "but at the same time I kind of hate him for this."

Like many other QAnon believers, Mackenzie's dad is opposed to the use of masks as a means of preventing the spread of the coronavirus. Mackenzie says her mother has even considered going to court to change his visitation rights "until he can wear his mask and until he's ready to protect his children."

Mackenzie says she doesn't want to stop seeing her dad, but it takes a toll on her mental health to be inundated with debunked theories about COVID-19 being fake and the deep state. She considered not seeing her dad for awhile, but decided not to go through with it. "I love him and he loves me. We still have a father-daughter bond, or whatever, but it's like there's a distance to it," she says.

QAnon is no longer just an American phenomenon; it's gone global, spreading around the world, including to the United Kingdom and Australia, according to *The Guardian*.

Yesenia, 20, from Costa Rica, asked for a pseudonym to protect her anonymity. Her experience is similar to Mackenzie's: As Yesenia's dad delves deeper into QAnon, she feels like she's losing him. She says it's particularly difficult because she's an only child, so she just has her mom and dad to turn to. Whether she's having a personal struggle or looking for advice, her dad is now "probably the last person" she will go to because his answers are always wrapped up in conspiracy theories.

Now she doesn't bother asking him for anything. "I don't want to waste my time with that," she says. Instead, she relies entirely on her mother. "You get used to not having your dad there to talk to," she adds. "That's the reality of it."

David Neiwert, a journalist who reports on domestic terrorism and recently published the book *Red Pill, Blue Pill: How to Counteract the Conspiracy Theories That Are Killing Us*, says he typically encounters parents who are trying to save their children from the depths of a conspiracy theory. Children trying to save their parents face an inherently more difficult journey. "They're going to have a bit harder time convincing their parents because they're in the position of being the person with less life experience," Neiwert explains.

Neiwert agrees with Miller-Idriss that you can't bring someone back from conspiratorial beliefs with facts and logic, because conspiracy theories are not built on facts or logic. "Those things don't matter to a theorist," he says. "What matters is the overall emotional narrative they get out of it. It's telling them the stories they want to hear."

What can motivate a conspiracy theorist to change their thinking, Neiwert explains, are the friendships and relationships they hold dear. If someone wants to change a conspiracy theorist's mind, it's beneficial to "find ways to deepen your relationship with them," he says, because that's the thing that can encourage them to change.

But even as Neiwert explains the possible paths to bring someone back from the edges of a conspiracy theory, he acknowledges that "some people go really far down the rabbit hole and become very volatile and difficult to deal with. Sometimes, your chances of success are about 1%, but people have to make those decisions to try anyway for themselves."

> *"Former believers who've extricated themselves have also taken to such subreddits to share their own stories, recounting what drew them in and providing tips and resources for those trying to get their family members out."*

Some People Who Believe in Conspiracy Theories Can Break Free from Their Beliefs

EJ Dickson

In the following viewpoint, EJ Dickson explores the stories of people who found themselves believing in and supporting the QAnon conspiracy, but who have since seen the misinformation for what it is and have removed themselves from the conspiracy. These people and others have taken to corners of the internet such as Reddit to share their stories of what ultimately brought them out. They also provide suggestions to others who are trying to get their own family members out. The subjects of the interviews discuss how they convinced other family members to believe the conspiracy theory and how they are attempting to get their own family members out now. EJ Dickson is a staff writer for Rolling Stone *covering culture.*

As you read, consider the following questions:

1. According to the viewpoint, how and why are conspiracy theories similar to team sports?
2. How can believing in a conspiracy theory like QAnon or Pizzagate feel empowering?
3. Instead of fact-checking, what should a person do if they have a friend or loved one embroiled in a conspiracy theory?

Jitarth Jadeja is a hirsute man in his early thirties, charming and jovial, speaking with equal effusiveness about economics and his baby niece. He's an atheist, pro-choice and pro-drug decriminalization, who supported Bernie Sanders in the 2016 primary. He doesn't seem like the kind of guy who would be deeply invested in a dangerous far-right conspiracy theory involving baby-eating Democrats and Hollywood actors. But for two and a half years, he says, that's exactly what he was.

"It's almost like a drug," he tells *Rolling Stone* from his parents' house in Sydney, Australia. "You read a Q drop and he tells you something, and you're like, 'Whoa dude, that's crazy'.... a hit of dopamine goes off in your brain, and you have to go in deeper and deeper and deeper in order to get that feeling again. When Q first started posting I felt like, 'Here is an explanation that, while it doesn't make sense, if it were true explains the situation better than the current explanations I'm getting.'"

QAnon is a loosely connected system of conspiracy theories and unfounded beliefs spawned by Q, an anonymous on forums like 8chan (now 8kun) claiming to have high-end military clearance within the Trump administration. QAnon adherents believe, among other things, in the existence of a deep state cabal of pedophiles and child traffickers led by prominent liberals like the Clintons, and that President Trump is lying in wait to arrest and execute his enemies.

QAnon Is a Drug

In 2017, after becoming enthralled with American politics while studying in the US, Australian Jitarth Jadeja fell under the influence of QAnon, a debunked and harmful online conspiracy theory. Jadeja said he was drawn into the web of its conspiracies when he started following fringe media figures like Alex Jones; online message boards like 4chan and 8chan further radicalized him.

"[QAnon is] just such a good story, you know, like this insider leaking secret government information," Jadeja told CBS News chief Washington correspondent Major Garrett in this week's episode of "The Takeout" podcast.

QAnon supporters vary in their beliefs, but the general conspiracy alleges former president Donald Trump is key to stopping a ring of Satan-worshipping pedophiles who run a child sex-trafficking operation. It centers around anonymous message board posts by "Q"—allegedly a government employee with a top-secret security clearance—and it ties in conspiracies involving President John F. Kennedy's assassination, school shootings, "Pizzagate" and the Mueller Report. And QAnon helped propagate former president Trump's so-called "Big Lie"—that the 2020 election was stolen from Mr. Trump.

Jadeja was a believer for two years, but has since disavowed the cult. He now moderates online forums for former QAnon supporters in search of help for themselves or loved ones who have become followers.

Recently, QAnon has gotten a great deal of attention in the media due to QAnon-promoting congressional candidates such as Republican nominees Marjorie Taylor Greene and Lauren Boebert, thus bringing the theory mainstream. It has also been linked to violence, such as the 2019 shooting of a Staten Island mob boss by a QAnon supporter and a Texas woman attacking two strangers with her car earlier this year because she believed them to be child traffickers. President Trump has refused to overtly discredit or reject QAnon ideology, to the delight of believers, whose primary goal is to win Trump's attention.

"It was absolutely a drug," Jadeja said of QAnon. "It just spirals out of control from there because like any drug, you need a bigger and bigger hit to get that high—which is why you need a bigger, more grandiose conspiracy theory."

Jadeja said he was addicted, "all day, every day for months, just looking and searching for that hit." By the time he was fully indoctrinated into the QAnon community, Jadeja said that he believed in some of its more outlandish theories, including one that claimed German chancellor Angela Merkel being Adolf Hitler's biological daughter.

But after he began investigating some of the outlandish claims made by "Q," Jadeja realized that it was all a fraud.

"It felt like in the space of one second, the entire universe collapsed in on me," Jadeja said about the moment he realized QAnon was composed of lies. "I felt like just a brain in a jar with no control... I didn't know what to think. I was almost like I was rebooting from the ground up."

Jadeja's biggest regret was indoctrinating his dad, who today remains a QAnon believer.

"That is the worst thing that I've ever done," Jadeja said. "So when we were in the cult together, it brought us very close in a way that had never happened before. And I was for the first time in my life, I felt like my dad was giving me a lot of respect."

His father's continued belief in QAnon has strained their relationship, he said.

"Former QAnon Believer Says Following the Conspiracy 'Was Absolutely a Drug,'" by Jake Rosen, CBS News, February 14, 2021.

"They desperately need a place to put their anger and a way to make sense of the world. Us versus them, the horrible bad guys, is something they all seem to cling to," says cult expert Diane Benscoter, who has spoken to numerous people whose loved ones are involved in QAnon. "The doctrine makes it easy to say, 'Clearly we have to make a stand against this,' and it feels really good to believe you're on the side of righteousness and saving children."

The mainstreaming of QAnon has also led to the advent of subreddits like r/QAnonCasualties and r/ReQuovery, for family members of QAnon believers to discuss the impact the ideology has had on their lives. Former believers who've extricated themselves have also taken to such subreddits to share their own stories, recounting what drew them in and providing tips and resources for those trying to get their family members out.

"I was disillusioned with the system, and seeing the system reward corruption, the idea that these people were so corrupt there was nothing they couldn't do wasn't that outlandish to me," says Lem, 26, a computer programmer in Columbus, Ohio.

Like Jadeja, Lem did not identify as conservative, and supported Sanders during the 2016 primary; his disgust with the liberal establishment after having seen Sanders passed over for Hillary Clinton at the 2016 Democratic National Convention is what led him to become obsessed with Pizzagate, the antecedent to QAnon, a conspiracy theory suggesting that Clinton and other Democratic operatives were running a child trafficking ring out of the basement of Comet Ping-Pong Pizza in Washington, D.C.

Anti-Clinton sentiment stoked by vloggers on YouTube set the stage for him to believe even the most outlandish claims proposed by Pizzagaters. It also helped, he says, that he grew up in an extremely religious Christian Baptist family (he says his father is still an ardent QAnon believer). "[Growing] up 18 years in that household played a role into my being primed believing something that was outlandish," he says. "[The] fact that you can have that kind of faith in certain things leads you to be open into believing certain things without there necessarily being proof."

Another common thread among the stories of former believers on Reddit is a history of mental illness. Jadeja had recently disconnected himself from many of his friends; he was isolated and intensely struggling with depression and undiagnosed bipolar II disorder. Because he was in graduate school, he also had a lot of time on his hands. "I was, I guess you could say, a prime candidate for Q to take a hold of me," he says.

Ivan, 26, who asked to be identified by a pseudonym for fear of getting doxxed, was struggling with anxiety and depression when he stumbled on Pizzagate in the subreddit r/cringeanarchy in

2016, right before Trump's election. Though r/cringeanarchy, which would later be banned, was a haven of far-right "edgy" content, "I was politically illiterate," though alienated and embittered, he recalls. Swapping theories about Pizzagate "wasn't about politics. It was about team sports. It was about cheering for this side, for Team Right." Scraping together bits of "evidence" whole cloth to support Pizzagate was not just fun, it was also empowering at a time when he was desperate to feel some semblance of control.

Ivan was conscious enough of how deranged his views sounded that he instinctively knew not to mention them to others—not, he says, that it would have helped. "I distinctly remember that if I read some article about this debunking or fact-checking, I would feel bored. I'd feel like, 'What am I reading here? They are just probably hiding the truth. It's not even worth the attention,'" he says. "From my own experience, when you get deep enough, any kind of fact-checking, it just flies right through you and you don't really capture the information at all."

Benscoter agrees that fact-checking is essentially useless. As difficult as it may be, she urges, those with loved ones deep into QAnon must refrain. "To try to make rational arguments is not going to work because they're not going to think rationally," she says. "You can throw rocks in it and try to make cracks," for instance, by asking the other person to consider the possibility that Q may not be who they claim to be. But arguing with a person who is not operating according to logic or reason "just makes them stand firmer," she says.

Instead, she advises people to try to appeal to their loved ones' "higher selves." "People who get involved in extremist mentality are usually really good people who care deeply about wanting to use their life for something bigger than themselves," she says. She urges loved ones of QAnon believers to approach the conversation by saying something like, "I know the reason you care so much about this is because you're a good person and I know you want to do right, but just consider the possibility that you are being lied to," or, "It would be a shame if you put all this good sincere energy in something that turns out to be a lie." "If they don't immediately argue back fervently, if they stop for a moment, that would be a sign of a crack" in their belief system, she says. It may take a long time for such cracks to emerge, but without them believers can't do the difficult work of setting off on the process of self-rediscovery and recovery from the false delusion of Q.

It took years for the cracks to emerge for Jadeja, who slowly started to realize that Q drops were laden with logical inconsistencies. A turning point for him was a follower asking Q to get Trump to say the term "tippy top" as proof of Trump's knowledge of the conspiracy; when Trump did say the phrase during a 2018 Easter egg roll speech, Q believers rejoiced, believing it to be confirmation that Q was real. Jadeja did some research and saw that Trump had said the phrase many times before. "That's when I realized this was all a very slick con," he says.

Today he views the rise of QAnon with abject horror, which is compounded by the fact that he'd also managed to rope his own father into the conspiracy. (Like Lem, Jadeja's father is still a true believer.) "It's gone out of control. And it continues to grow out of control. And they're not going away. Even if Trump loses, they're not going to go away, they'll just look at it as part of the conspiracy," he says. He sees speaking out about his own involvement with the cult of QAnon as a form of penance—even as he worries it may be too late to curb its toxic, potentially lethal influence.

"Any time you dehumanize any part or segment of the population to such a low level, to the lowest level you can go, people are happy on the opposite side to do the worst against them," he says of QAnon believers' views of Trump's enemies. "That's the real danger here—not that [QAnon adherents] will get into the Senate. When you frame your opponents [as subhuman], you won't just watch them burn. You'll be happy about it."

> *"A group of conspiracy theorists is attractive because it is seen as holding a superior truth against others—effectively, a knowledge high ground."*

Steps Can Be Taken to Prevent Belief in Conspiracy Theories Before It Can Take Root

Thomas Roulet

In the following viewpoint, Thomas Roulet argues that conspiracy theories and general misinformation thrive under certain conditions and can be symptomatic of several societal problems. He believes such theories can be combatted early by teaching critical thinking in schools and also by reinforcing universal values to provide a strong identity to people who lack one. The author cites examples and studies that, at least in their early stages, seem promising. Thomas Roulet is senior lecturer in organization theory and fellow in sociology at Girton College, University of Cambridge. His work has been featured in various media, including the Economist, *the* Financial Times, *the* Washington Post, *and BBC Radio.*

"To Combat Conspiracy Theories Teach Critical Thinking—and Community Values," by Thomas Roulet, The Conversation, October 2, 2020, https://theconversation.com/to-combat-conspiracy-theories-teach-critical-thinking-and-community-values-147314.

As you read, consider the following questions:

1. According to the author, how do politicans benefit from taking outrageous stances?
2. In what situations can conspiracy theories thrive, according to the viewpoint?
3. What universal values did Finland focus on in an effort to combat conspiracy theories and misinformation?

In the era of social media, conspiracy theories feel more prominent and prevalent than ever before. Most recently, the high level of uncertainty surrounding the COVID-19 pandemic, combined with people's desire to make sense of a new reality, spawned a range of new conspiracy theories while also reinforcing existing ones. These fuelled the spread of misinformation about the virus, giving succour to anti-mask groups.

Meanwhile, the US presidential election is also awash with conspiracy theories. Perhaps most prominent among these is QAnon, whose followers push a range of false ideas and claims about the Democratic Party. QAnon followers have been tacitly endorsed by Donald Trump—who the conspiracy theory conveniently sees as their saviour.

In my recent book, *The Power of Being Divisive*, I explain how politicians benefit from taking the most radical and outrageous stances. They can capitalise on the claims made by conspiracy theorists, to antagonise certain groups, bolster their identity and, ultimately, convert them into loyal voters.

Research shows that people buy into conspiracy theories when times are stressful and uncertain. In these situations people tend to make less accurate judgements about the validity of the information they are given. But believing in conspiracy theories also makes people feel part of something bigger than themselves, and provides them with a tribe to belong to.

In my book, I discuss potential solutions to address both these problems at once. In particular, I build on Finland's recent experience of combating the spread of fake news and conspiracy theories by teaching critical thinking in school.

Get 'Em While They're Young

Lots of governments fund specific agencies to fight for the truth and try and counter the spread of conspiracy theories. The US for example, has the Global Engagement Center, which tries to engage with attempts to manipulate opinion on social media by sourcing their origins and in some cases putting out counter-messaging. But the level of information and speed with which it can spread on social media—along with a president who peddles conspiracy theories—has made their mission difficult, to say the least.

What's more, conspiracy theories thrive on distrust of the government. As a consequence, these official agencies often struggle to contain the spread of fake news.

Finland took a significantly different approach. After seeing the damage done by the fake news spread in neighbouring Russia, the Finnish government set up a plan to teach critical thinking in secondary school in 2014. It integrated media literacy into the curriculum and got students to exercise their critical thinking when collecting information on a specific topic. The source is assessed, and so is the content.

Students are also trained to critically evaluate statistics and numbers. These can be particularly confusing or intimidating to critique—and we naturally tend to give them legitimacy. But the Finnish experience proves that giving citizens the confidence to debunk conspiracy theories themselves is more effective than providing them with the right information.

The Complementary Role of Universal Values

But another challenge is looming—and critical thinking is not enough. Followers of conspiracy theories, whether they believe in QAnon or that the world is flat, are often drawn to the community element of conspiracy theories. They feel like they belong to a select group, which makes them feel unique and special. They believe they have access to exclusive and well-guarded knowledge, which makes them feel distinctive.

These ideas are at the centre of social identity theory in psychology research. This is the idea that our perception of ourselves as individuals is driven by the groups we belong to and the identity that they have. A group of conspiracy theorists is attractive because it is seen as holding a superior truth against others—effectively, a knowledge high ground.

Finnish authorities understood this. Their secondary school programme also focused on reminding pupils of the important universal values upheld by Finnish society. These include fairness, the rule of law, respect for others' differences, openness and freedom. Together, these are a powerful lens to exercise their critical thinking—students are called to make sense of information with these values in mind.

Ultimately, students are reminded of all the good things about being Finnish and that they already belong to group with a positive identity. This throws the identity benefits of believing in conspiracy theories into question. Plus, their Finnish identity becomes more salient as they question and identify fake news. Critical thinking and countering misinformation is what makes them part of a group they can be proud of.

Of course, this is difficult to measure but the evidence so far suggests Finland's approach is working. A 2019 study found that Finnish pupils are much better at identifying fake news than their US counterparts. But the real benefits will take years to study, not least because Finland's programme only really ramped up in the last couple of years.

The spread of conspiracy theories will not be stopped by simply giving younger generations the right training to engage in fact-checking, or collect evidence-based information. The reality of conspiracy theory groups is that they represent fragmented parts of our society—their very existence is made possible by social exclusion. So we must teach critical thinking alongside ensuring people feel part of a broader community.

> *"The concept of deprogramming rests on the idea that people do not choose alternative beliefs... When people call for QAnon believers to be deprogrammed, they are implicitly denying that followers exercised choice in accepting QAnon beliefs."*

QAnon Believers Cannot Be Deprogrammed

Paul Thomas

In the following viewpoint, Paul Thomas argues that the idea that QAnon believers and other conspiracy theorists can be deprogrammed is largely a myth. This is because most people who believe in QAnon do so willingly and without coercion. The author also contends that to insist that these people can simply be deprogrammed absolves them of personal responsibility. Paul Thomas is professor of religious studies and department chair in the Department of Philosophy and Religious Studies at Radford University.

As you read, consider the following questions:

1. Where did the modern concept of brainwashing begin?
2. What is exit counseling?
3. How is social influence different from brainwashing?

"'Deprogramming' QAnon Followers Ignores Free Will and Why They Adopted the Beliefs in the First Place," by Paul Thomas, The Conversation, April 14, 2021, https://theconversation.com/deprogramming-qanon-followers-ignores-free-will-and-why-they-adopted-the-beliefs-in-the-first-place-158372.

Recent calls to deprogram QAnon conspiracy followers are steeped in discredited notions about brainwashing. As popularly imagined, brainwashing is a coercive procedure that programs new long-term personality changes. Deprogramming, also coercive, is thought to undo brainwashing.

As a professor of religious studies who has written and taught about alternative religious movements, I believe such deprogramming conversations do little to help us understand why people adopt QAnon beliefs. A deprogramming discourse fails to understand religious recruitment and conversion and excuses those spreading QAnon beliefs from accountability.

A Brief Brainwashing History

Deprogramming, a method thought to reverse extreme psychological manipulation, can't be understood apart from the concept of brainwashing.

The modern concept of brainwashing has its origin in Chinese experiments with American prisoners of war during the Korean War. Coercive physical and psychological methods were employed in an attempt to plant Communist beliefs in the minds of American POWs. To determine whether brainwashing was possible, the CIA then launched its own secret mind-control program in the 1950s called MK-ULTRA.

By the late 1950s researchers were already casting doubt on brainwashing theory. The anti-American behavior of captured Americans was best explained by temporary compliance owing to torture. This is akin to false confessions made under extreme duress.

Still, books like *The Manchurian Candidate*, released in 1959, and *A Clockwork Orange*, released in 1962—both of which were turned into movies and heavily featured themes of brainwashing—reinforced the concept in popular culture. To this day, the language of brainwashing and deprogramming is applied to groups holding controversial beliefs—from fundamentalist Mormons to passionate Trump supporters.

In the 1970s and 1980s, brainwashing was used to explain why people would join new religious movements like Jim Jones' Peoples Temple or the Unification Church.

Seeking guardianship of adult children in these groups, parents cited the belief that members were brainwashed to justify court-ordered conservatorship. With guardianship orders in hand, they sought help from cult deprogrammers like Ted Patrick. Deprogrammers were notorious for kidnapping, isolating and harassing adults in an effort to reverse perceived cult brainwashing.

For a time, US courts accepted brainwashing testimony despite the pseudo-scientific nature of the theory. It turns out that research on coercive conversion failed to support brainwashing theory. Several professional organizations, including the American Psychological Association, have filed legal briefs against brainwashing testimony. Others argued that deprogramming practices violated civil rights.

In 1995 the coercive deprogramming method was litigated again in *Scott v. Ross*. The jury awarded the plaintiff nearly US$5 million in total damages. This bankrupted the co-defending Cult Awareness Network, a popular resource at the time for those seeking deprogramming services.

"Exit Counseling"

Given this tarnished history, coercive deprogramming evolved into "exit counseling." Unlike deprogramming, exit counseling is voluntary and resembles an intervention or talk therapy.

One of the most visible self-styled exit counselors is former deprogrammer Rick Alan Ross, the executive director of the Cult Education Institute and defendant in *Scott v. Ross*. Through frequent media appearances, people including Ross and Steve Hassan, founder of the Freedom of Mind Resource Center, continue to contribute to the mind-control and deprogramming discourse in popular culture.

These "cult-recovery experts," some of whom were involved with the old deprogramming model, are now being used for QAnon deprogramming advice.

Some, like Ross, advocate for a more aggressive intervention approach. Others, like Hassan, offer a gentler approach that includes active listening. Cult specialist Pat Ryan says he only recommends intervention after a thorough assessment in conjunction with a mental health professional.

Choice vs. Coercion

Despite the pivot to exit counseling, the language of deprogramming persists. The concept of deprogramming rests on the idea that people do not choose alternative beliefs. Instead, beliefs that are deemed too deviant for mainstream culture are thought to result from coercive manipulation by nefarious entities like cult leaders. When people call for QAnon believers to be deprogrammed, they are implicitly denying that followers exercised choice in accepting QAnon beliefs.

This denies the personal agency and free will of those who became QAnon enthusiasts, and shifts the focus to the programmer. It can also relieve followers of responsibility for perpetuating QAnon beliefs.

As I suggested in an earlier article, and as evident in the QAnon influence on the Jan. 6, 2021, capital insurrection, QAnon beliefs can be dangerous. I believe those who adopt and perpetuate these beliefs ought to be held responsible for the consequences.

This isn't to say that people are not subject to social influence. However, social influence is a far cry from the systematic, mind-swiping, coercive, robotic imagery conjured up by brainwashing.

Admittedly, what we choose to believe is constrained by the types of influences we face. Those restraints emerge from our social and economic circumstances. In the age of social media, we are also constrained by algorithms that influence the media we consume. Further examination of these issues in relation to the development of QAnon would prove fruitful.

But applying a brainwashing and deprogramming discourse limits our potential to understand the grievances of the QAnon community. To suggest "they were temporarily out of their minds" relieves followers of the conspiracy of responsibility and shelters the rest of society from grappling with uncomfortable social realities.

To understand the QAnon phenomenon, I believe analysts must dig deeply into the social, economic and political factors that influence the adoption of QAnon beliefs.

Periodical and Internet Sources Bibliography

The following articles have been selected to supplement the diverse views presented in this chapter.

Karen Douglas, "Speaking of Psychology: Why People Believe in Conspiracy Theories, with Karen Douglas, PhD," American Psychological Association, January 2021. https://www.apa.org/research/action/speaking-of-psychology/conspiracy-theories

John Ehrenreich, "Why People Believe in Conspiracy Theories," Slate, January 11, 2021. https://slate.com/technology/2021/01/conspiracy-theories-coronavirus-fake-psychology.html

Graig Graziosi, "Cult Deprogrammers Inundated with Requests to Help People Lost in Trump Election, QAnon Conspiracy Theories," *The Independent*, March 3, 2021. https://www.independent.co.uk/news/world/americas/us-politics/cult-trump-election-qanon-conspiracy-theories-b1812078.html

Joe Hagan, "So Many Great, Educated People Were Brainwashed; Can Trump's Cult of Followers Be Deprogrammed?" *Vanity Fair*, January 21, 2021. https://www.vanityfair.com/news/2021/01/can-trumps-cult-of-followers-be-deprogrammed

Izabella Kaminska, "The 'Game Theory' in the QAnon Conspiracy Theory," *Financial Times*, October 16, 2020. https://www.ft.com/content/74f9d20f-9ff9-4fad-808f-c7e4245a1725

Jessica Kent, "Machine Learning Tracks Evolution of COVID-19 Misinformation," Health IT Analytics, April 21, 2021. https://healthitanalytics.com/news/machine-learning-tacks-evolution-of-covid-19-misinformation

Laura Mullane, "New AI Tool Tracks Evolution of COVID-19 Conspiracy Theories on Social Media," Los Alamos National Laboratory, April 19, 2021. https://www.lanl.gov/discover/news-release-archive/2021/April/0419-ai-tool-tracks-conspiracy-theories.php

Timothy R. Rangherlini, "An AI Tool Can Distinguish Between a Conspiracy Theory and a True Conspiracy—It Comes Down to How Easily the Story Falls Apart," The Conversation, November 13, 2020. https://theconversation.com/an-ai-tool-can-distinguish

-between-a-conspiracy-theory-and-a-true-conspiracy-it-comes-down-to-how-easily-the-story-falls-apart-146282

Kaleigh Rogers and Jasmine Mithani, "Why People Fall for Conspiracy Theories," FiveThirtyEight, June 15, 2021. https://fivethirtyeight.com/features/why-people-fall-for-conspiracy-theories/

Jake Rosen, "Former QAnon Believer Says Following the Conspiracy 'Was Absolutely a Drug,'" CBS News, February 14, 2021. https://www.cbsnews.com/news/qanon-conspiracy-believer-drug/

Ari Shapiro, "Experts in Cult Deprogramming Step In to Help Believers in Conspiracy Theories," NPR, March 2, 2021. https://www.npr.org/2021/03/02/972970805/experts-in-cult-deprogramming-step-in-to-help-believers-in-conspiracy-theories

Stevens Institute of Technology, "Stevens-Developed Artificial Intelligence That Detects Fake News Could Be Used to Identify Conspiracy Theories," January 7, 2021. https://www.stevens.edu/news/stevens-developed-artificial-intelligence-detects-fake-news-could-be-used-identify-conspiracy

For Further Discussion

Chapter 1

1. What are the dangers of the anti-Semitic rhetoric found in the QAnon conspiracy theory? How are non-Christian religions similarly susceptible to conspiracy theories?
2. What can be done to regulate QAnon and other conspiracy theories on more fringe websites like Telegram?

Chapter 2

1. What else can social media companies do to stem the flood of misinformation online? As private companies, are they obligated to act at all?
2. Is having a QAnon believer in Congress like Marjorie Taylor Greene similar or different from having Congresspeople who fall on the more radical-leaning side of the left?

Chapter 3

1. If the media had delegitimized the birtherism conspiracy theory, could the rise of QAnon have been avoided? Why or why not?
2. What are potential reasons why the US government would bother to declassify many conspiracies to the rest of the world?

Chapter 4

1. What are other ways in which people who have family members embroiled in conspiracy theories like QAnon can seek help?
2. What are the potential negative ramifications to using AI and machine learning as a tool to identify misinformation online?

Organizations to Contact

The editors have compiled the following list of organizations concerned with the issues debated in this book. The descriptions are derived from materials provided by the organizations. All have publications or information available for interested readers. The list was compiled on the date of publication of the present volume; the information provided here may change. Be aware that many organizations take several weeks or longer to respond to inquiries, so allow as much time as possible.

American Civil Liberties Union

1313 West 8th Street
Los Angeles, CA 90017
(213) 977-9500
email: info@aclusocal.org
website: https://www.aclu.org/

The ACLU has evolved from a small group of idealists into the nation's premier defender of the rights enshrined in the US Constitution. With more than 1.7 million members, 500 staff attorneys, thousands of volunteer attorneys, and offices throughout the nation, the ACLU of today continues to fight government abuse and to vigorously defend individual freedoms, including speech and religion, a woman's right to choose, the right to due process, citizens' rights to privacy, and much more. The ACLU stands up for these rights even when the cause is unpopular, and sometimes when nobody else will. While not always in agreement on every issue, Americans have come to count on the ACLU for its unyielding dedication to principle. The ACLU has become so ingrained in American society that it is hard to imagine an America without it.

Anti-Defamation League

605 Third Avenue
New York, NY 10158-3650
(212) 885-7700
email: www.adl.org/contact
website: https://www.adl.org/

ADL is a leading anti-hate organization that was founded in 1913 in response to an escalating climate of anti-Semitism and bigotry. Today, ADL is the first call when acts of anti-Semitism occur and continues to fight all forms of hate. A global leader in exposing extremism, delivering anti-bias education, and fighting hate online, ADL's ultimate goal is a world in which no group or individual suffers from bias, discrimination, or hate.

Center for Strategic & International Studies

1616 Rhode Island Avenue NW
Washington, DC 20036
(202) 887-0200
email: webmaster@csis.org
website: https://www.csis.org/

The Center for Strategic and International Studies (CSIS) is a bipartisan, nonprofit policy research organization dedicated to advancing practical ideas to address the world's greatest challenges. CSIS's purpose is to define the future of national security. It is guided by a distinct set of values—nonpartisanship, independent thought, innovative thinking, cross-disciplinary scholarship, integrity and professionalism, and talent development. CSIS's values work in concert toward the goal of making real-world impact.

Center for the Study of Hate and Extremism

5000 University Parkway
San Bernardino, CA 92407
(909) 537-5000
email: Blevin8@aol.com
website: https://www.csusb.edu/hate-and-extremism-center/about-us

The Center for the Study of Hate and Extremism at California State University, San Bernardino, is a nonpartisan research and policy center that examines the ways that bigotry, advocacy of extreme methods, or terrorism, both domestic and international, deny civil or human rights to people on the basis of race, ethnicity, religion, gender, sexual orientation, disability, or other relevant status characteristics. The center seeks to aid scholars, community activists, government officials, law enforcement, the media, and others with objective information to aid them in their examination and implementation of law, education, and policy.

Cult Education Institute

1977 N. Olden Avenue
Trenton, NJ 08618
(609) 396-6684
email: info@culteducation.com
website: https://culteducation.com/

The Cult Education Institute (CEI) is a nonprofit, tax-exempt 501(c)(3) organization devoted to public education and research. CEI's mission is to study destructive cults and controversial groups and movements, and to provide a broad range of information and services easily accessible to the public for assistance and educational purposes online. CEI maintains a large, public online database to assist researchers, the media, professionals, and those concerned with accurate information about various cults, groups, and movements and related issues of interest. CEI is an institutional member of both the New Jersey Library Association and American Library Association.

The Heritage Foundation

214 Massachusetts Avenue NE
Washington, DC 20002-4999
(800) 546-2843
email: info@heritage.org
website: https://www.heritage.org/

The Heritage Foundation advocates for individual liberty, limited government, free enterprise, traditional American values, and a strong national defense to protect it all. Out of the over 8,000 think tanks that exist worldwide, the Heritage Foundation has consistently been ranked no. 1 in the world for its impact on public policy. Its renowned experts spend each day developing solutions to America's biggest issues—from creating more jobs, improving the economy, and building stronger families to securing our borders, making health care more affordable, and so much more.

Online News Association

1111 North Capitol Street NE
Second Floor
Washington, DC 20002
email: support@journalists.org
website: https://journalists.org/

The Online News Association is a leader in the rapidly changing world of journalism, a catalyst for innovation in story-telling across all platforms, a resource for journalists seeking guidance and growth, and a champion of best practices through training, awards, and community outreach. Since 1999, ONA has been at the forefront of a truly revolutionary age in digital media. The programs and services it provides help digital journalists in news organizations around the globe and across the corporate, independent, and nonprofit sectors adapt to the changing environment. Its mission, inspiring innovation and excellence among digital journalists to better serve the public, has never been more important.

Pew Research Center

16165 L Street NW
Suite 800
Washington, DC 20036
(202) 419-4300
email: info@pewresearch.org
website: https://www.pewresearch.org/

Pew Research Center is a nonpartisan fact tank that informs the public about the issues, attitudes, and trends shaping the world. It conduct public opinion polling, demographic research, content analysis, and other data-driven social science research. It does not take policy positions. It generates a foundation of facts that enriches the public dialogue and supports sound decision-making. It is nonprofit, nonpartisan, and nonadvocacy. It values independence, objectivity, accuracy, rigor, humility, transparency, and innovation.

The Poynter Institute

801 Third Street South
St. Petersburg, FL 33701
(727) 821-9494
email: info@poynter.org
website: https://www.poynter.org/

Founded in 1975, Poynter is an inspirational place but also a practical one, connecting the varied crafts of journalism to its higher mission and purpose. From person-to-person coaching and intensive hands-on seminars to interactive online courses and media reporting, Poynter helps journalists sharpen skills and elevate storytelling throughout their careers.

Society of Professional Journalists

3909 N. Meridian Street
Suite 200
Indianapolis, IN 46208
(317) 927-8000
email: lindah@spj.org
website: https://www.spj.org/

The Society of Professional Journalists is the nation's most broad-based journalism organization, dedicated to encouraging the free practice of journalism and stimulating high standards of ethical behavior. Founded in 1909 as Sigma Delta Chi, SPJ promotes the free flow of information vital to a well-informed citizenry through the daily work of its roughly 6,000 members, works to inspire and educate current and future journalists through professional development, and protects First Amendment guarantees of freedom of speech and press through its advocacy efforts.

Index

A

B

C

Bibliography of Books

Sinan Aral. *The Hype Machine: How Social Media Disrupts Our Elections, Our Economy, and Our Health—and How We Must Adapt*. New York, NY: Currency, 2020.

Eric Berkowitz. *Dangerous Ideas*. New York, NY: Penguin Random House, 2021.

Peter Block. *Community*. New York, NY: Penguin Random House, 2018.

Allum Bokhari. *#DELETED: Big Tech's Battle to Erase a Movement and Subvert Democracy*. Boston, MA: Little, Brown and Company, 2021.

Ashley "Dotty" Charles. *Outraged: Why Everyone Is Shouting and No One Is Talking*. London, UK: Bloomsbury Publishing, 2020.

Tom Cutler. *It's a Conspiracy! The World's Wildest Conspiracy Theories. What They Don't Want You to Know, and Why the Truth Is Out There*. New York, NY: HarperCollins Publishers, 2021.

Christian Fuchs. *Communicating COVID-19: Everyday Life, Digital Capitalism, and Conspiracy Theories in Pandemic Times*. Bingley, UK: Emerald Group Publishing, 2021.

Eric Hoffer. *True Believer Thoughts on the Nature of Mass Movements*. New York, NY: Harper & Brothers, 1951.

Brian Jefferson. *Digitize and Punish: Racial Criminalization in the Digital Age*. Minneapolis, MN: University of Minnesota Press, 2020.

Carol Leonnig. *I Alone Can Fix It: Donald J. Trump's Catastrophic Final Year*. New York, NY: Penguin Random House, 2021.

Jill Lepore. *If*
the Future

Ed Miliband.
Vintage P

Douglas Mur
Identity. I

Barack Obam
Publishin

Frank Pasqu
Expertise
2020.

Mike Rothsc
Random